EAT TO HEALTH AND WELLNESS ON AN AFRICAN DIET

My Food-To-Wellness Journey And Useful Tips.

Olayinka Flo Falana

All rights reserved. No part of this publication may be reproduced, stored in a retrieval system or transmitted, in any form or by any means without the prior permission in writing of the author or as expressly permitted by law, or under terms agreed with the appropriate reprographics rights organisation.

Enquiries concerning reproduction outside the scope of the above should be sent to the author. You must not circulate this book in any other binding or cover, and you must impose this same condition on any acquirer.

All images used are stock images and have been used with permission.

Printed in the United Kingdom

Copyright © 2021 Olayinka Flo Falana

Produced by Bytels Publishing.

Disclaimer

This book is about my journey to wellness and is not intended to replace the advice of your doctor, or other trained health practitioners. If you have any health issue I recommend you seek professional help. The information in this book must not be substituted for professional advice.

DEDICATION

In Loving Memory

This book is dedicated to my mother, Idowu Christianah.

I also remember my dear friends, Titilola Akinboro and Oluwayemisi Soile.

Rest in Peace.

ACKNOWLEDGMENT

I thank God Almighty, through Jesus Christ for a sound mind, a fit body and a vibrant spirit, without which this book would not have been possible.

I recognize that throughout Africa, regardless of tribe or tongue we pretty much eat the same foods with variations in spices, cooking methods, and I acknowledge that we are the same.

I appreciate my Dad, my brother George Falana, and my children, Corey and Modupe for their constant support and love.

I appreciate the members of the 'Eat to Health' WhatsApp group for their support and contributions. You are all awesome. Thank you

I thank you, Koito for sharing your pictures with me.

I acknowledge the help of many people who have contributed to the completion and success of this book, especially those who took the time to make YouTube videos.

I thank John Bergman, D.C, and Eric Berg for the wealth of information about how the body functions and how to maintain wellness. I also thank Barbara O'Neil for sharing her experiences and useful tips on herbal remedies.

I thank Fafa Gilbert of 'Ndudu by Fafa', Flo Chinyere of 'All Nigerian Recipes', 'Shine with Plants', and Don Imran Family Kitchen for sharing tasty recipes on YouTube. I also appreciate Mark Weins who travels the world to eat. Thank you for showing us world cuisines in colour.

I appreciate friends who believed in my skills and encouraged me to write. I thank Jimi Sotimehin, and Funke Oduntan for breathing down my neck, constantly hounding me to write.

To all, I say thank you!

TABLE OF CONTENTS

INTRODUCTION 1

THE POWER OF NUTRITION 14

KEYS TO HEALTH 31

EAT AFRICAN-NUTRIENT RICH INDIGENOUS
CROPS AND PLANTS 44

PRESSING ISSUES: WHAT'S NEXT? 62

HOME REMEDIES 67

BE PROACTIVE 84

FOOD COMBINATION SAMPLES 107

CONCLUSION 131

REFERENCES 134

INTRODUCTION

"Those who are well have no need of a physician, but those who are sick"

Jesus Christ (Mark 2:17)

Watching loved ones battle with sickness is disheartening; it weighs down our hearts, affects us physically and emotionally. It makes us feel helpless. We pray, we hope, we expend energy and resources; sometimes they get better, but sometimes we need to plan a funeral. Either way, sickness and diseases is something we all dread that's why the pharmaceutical industry is the most profitable industry on earth. Indeed, health is the major wealth we all desire.

What if I present to you a case for nutrition as a way to health? It sounds implausible, yet it is so true. It is hard to believe that nutrition is a tool in the medicine cabinet because we all eat, and find it hard to avoid diseases. What if we have been eating the wrong kinds of foods, or we are guilty of gluttony? What if we have not been eating enough and end up being nutrient deficient?

Diseases are not only caused by nutritional deficiencies, they are also caused by toxicities in the body. Environmental toxins in the air, our food supply and water are also responsible for ill-health. The good news is that whatever way the body becomes sick, nutritional science has proven that wellness can be restored because our bodies are self-healing and self-restoring as long as we provide them with the fuel essential for the regenerative and restorative process.

Despite the unbelief in nutrition as a weapon against ill health, there are many anecdotal pieces of evidence and scientific studies that prove that diseases can be prevented and reversed with diet and lifestyle change. Visit PubMed website and see for yourself how many studies pop up in the search engine when you plug in 'Whole Foods Plant-based'-

(https://pubmed.ncbi.nlm.nih.gov/)

In a blog post by Longevity technology *(https://longevity.technology/lifespan-is-120-really)*, the authors state that"...on average, middle-aged people today can expect to live 120 years", which corroborates the words in Genesis 6 v 3 "his days shall be hundred and twenty years". Therefore, my goal is for everyone who reads this book to get to the point where they will not need a physician, yet enjoy great health and vitality till their 120 years expiration date.

This goal of great health and longevity might seem outlandish, however, it is plausible looking at the diet and lifestyle of whole foods plant-based proponents, such as Caldwell B. Esselstyn, an American physician, T. Colin Campbell, an American biochemist, Eric L. Adams, an American politician, and Mike Adams (Health Ranger) to mention a few. Eric Adams was able to reverse type-2 diabetes within six months of switching to a vegan whole foods plant-based diet. Mike Adams (Health Ranger), overcame type-2 diabetes by educating himself about nutrition; stating in the documentary, 'The Truth About Cancer', that he hadn't visited a doctor in ten years, and enjoyed great health. He attributed his wellness to a healthy diet and regular exercise.

After combing through many books, watching hundreds of hours of videos on health and nutrition for the past nine years and listening to amazing recovery stories, I am motivated to compile what I have learned throughout the years.

I particularly focused on the African diet because all the information garnered from videos and books did not address the African palette or lifestyle, neither did garnered information mention African indigenous crops and foods as superfoods, yet African foods mainly consist of plant-based whole foods. The problem with malnutrition and unhealthy diets among Africans is because we don't eat a varied diet from a range of crops and plants. We tend to focus on a limited number of food choices, such as wheat, soybeans, cowpeas, corn and potatoes, staples that form the basis for processed foods. Our markets brim with sugary drinks and beverages, artificial flavour enhancers, processed flour and their by-products, and bulked up fruits like tomato puree.

Television commercials advertise sugar-loaded beverages as health foods, encouraging us to feed our children with these products. Little wonder today children as young as six years old are beginning to reach puberty; some girls as young as eight years are menstruating.

Another problem is the idea that animal flesh and milk are the only sources of protein. Protein is also available in plants, but because many people don't know they feel compelled to add meat, fish, and eggs to every meal that amounts to an over-indulgence in these foods, and they end up diseased. For instance, overindulgence in red meat is implicated in the risk for type-2 diabetes, coronary heart disease, stroke, and colorectal cancer.

A Nigerian adage within the Yoruba people encapsulates my message in one statement:

"What we eat are the diseases in our bodies".

In Africa, we have been made to believe that medication is the answer to all that ails our health. When it comes to introducing a new drug to the market, like a drug for diabetes, Africa is a lucrative market. We are discouraged from using our local herbs because according to many, it is dangerous to our organs. Yet, it is a known fact that prescription medication often comes with unwanted side effects. In the United States of America and other countries, thousands of people die annually due to adverse drug reactions. Many have become sick from using the right amount of prescription medication, and some have died. Allopathic medicine recognises the phenomenon that they termed it: 'iatrogenic' diseases (defined as a ***disease*** induced by a drug prescribed by a physician)
https://jamanetwork.com/journals/jamainternalmedicine

The question remains: are pharmaceutical medications the true solution to our health problems? Is it health care or sick maintenance? For instance, it has been proven through anecdotal evidence that diabetes can be reversed by returning to basics. Cutting out processed foods and sugary beverages, eating the right amount of animal protein based on body weight, making plant-based whole foods a part of the diet, with exercise, reverses diabetes.

Since I am proudly African, I decided to research foods original to us. Besides, in trying to adapt some of the recipes in the books that I read to meet the African palette, I realized it would be cumbersome to follow the protocols for effective results.

My objective is to build up an argument for a diet and lifestyle change with the hope that by the end of reading this book, you are convinced that nutrition is the solution to many of your health problems, an under-utilized powerful weapon in the arsenal of healthcare. I am greatly encouraged to show on the pages of this book that Africa is blessed indeed, and if we would dare to change a few things regarding how we prepare and combine our meals, we would be able to reverse diseases and maintain wellness.

My Argument

The world has become a global village connected by the internet and social media. We globally share similar experiences, for instance, 360 million people worldwide are dealing with diabetes and other chronic diseases. Cancer UK predicts that one in two people will get cancer in their lifetime. The global pandemic has claimed many lives; we are advised to wash hands, cover our noses and mouths, and stay away from friends and family, which I see as temporary solutions to an enduring problem because we are social beings. I strongly believe that life is lived from the inside out, and we are designed to live in sync with our environment; all that is needed is for us to master our environment. To master your environment, a basic understanding of plants and nutrition are essential *https://www.youtube.com/watch?v=LfO2CBruqu8*

In 2018 a Nigerian newspaper, 'The Punch', reported that over four million Nigerians are affected by diabetes. In this report, Dr Olufemi Fasanmade said that mortality rates for diabetes were higher than HIV, malaria and tuberculosis combined! He further reported that a third of patients who visited a hospital where he worked, presented with stroke, heart failure, or kidney failure exacerbated by diabetes.

According to W.H.O. reports, cancer rates in Nigeria have doubled over the last twenty years. The report is a true reflection of my personal experiences and the experiences of many others. Besides rising cancer rates, there are also rising cases of auto-immune diseases, and other metabolic syndromes. True to the report, within two years I lost three close friends to the ravaging effects of different types of cancer; that is excluding reports of family and friends of colleagues and acquaintances who are either battling cancer or have died from cancer and other metabolic diseases. However, despite the cost-effectiveness and anecdotal evidence that a whole foods plant-based diet is a powerful tool in the medicine cabinet, not much has been said in the area of nutrition, an ignored area of science.

For example, a relative in Nigeria learned she had diabetes when a wound was slow in healing. She was able to reverse type-2 diabetes by changing her food combination, and by adding herbs to her diet. It has been four years since her diagnosis, and her blood sugar readings are always within normal ranges. She told me her doctor was surprised at the transformation because he had never seen anyone reverse type-2 diabetes.

EAT TO HEALTH AND WELLNESS ON AN AFRICAN DIET

A Google search on nutrition as science defines it as a study of the physiological process of nutrition that interprets the nutrients and other phytochemical substances in food, and how it relates to health and diseases, wellness maintenance, growth, and reproduction.

For instance, in regards to reproduction, a small town in a Nigerian state is popularly known for having a set of twins in about 95 % of households. Though their diet has not been studied, it is theorized that a diet based on the local tuber (yam), and okra could be responsible for the high level of fertility in the town. I would love to one day conduct a scientific study on reproductive health, drawing my sample population from the 'Town of Twins', the people in Igboora, Oyo state, Nigeria.

My wellness journey began when I faced health challenges and my doctor told me point blank that she could not help me; the only solution was for me to be on medication for the rest of my life. I bought books on nutrition, watched videos on YouTube about health and wellness, and daily learnt something new about food, hormones and how it affects our health. I binged on health documentaries while cooking and cleaning. I took copious notes, writing on napkins, envelopes, and whatever I could scribble on. I was amazed at the wealth of information out there in the cyber world. Information that I never heard emanate from the box in my living room. My moribund television set sat languidly on its stand in the living room. Each time I walked past it, I simply kissed my teeth and brow-beat the inanimate object occupying valuable space until it ended up in a corner of my room, and eventually in the trash.

In the same year, a bosom friend was diagnosed with breast cancer. I was happy to share with her the wealth of information I had learned throughout the months. At that point, I only heard of cases of cancer, but this time, cancer had inched close to home.

My friend went through the traditional treatment of "cut, poison and burn", surgery, chemotherapy and radiation; family and friends were ecstatic to hear that she was cancer free. To celebrate her newness of life, my dear friend made it a point to weekly visit an ice cream parlour. Her oncologist had told her that diet had little or nothing to do with cancer because the cancer was a case of too much Estrogen causing cell multiplication. Based on what I had learned, I strongly disagreed with her, but since I didn't have a medical degree, to her, I didn't have any authority.

Fast forward two years to date, my bosom friend had difficulty raising her arm on the side where she'd had the mastectomy. A couple of tests later showed that cancer had returned. I loved my friend so much that I took a short course in nutrition to help with her treatment, especially in the area of her diet. We constantly locked horns when it came to her food choices because in my nutrition course I learned that breast cancer, amongst other types of cancers and diseases, was associated with diet and lifestyle.

My friend's next line of traditional cancer treatment was brutal. Her oncologist took out more lymph nodes since there was nothing left to chop off; pumped her with chemotherapy to the point that she needed regular blood transfusions. In my layman's opinion, regular blood transfusions didn't seem sustainable; I wondered what her bone marrow was doing. Had it gone to sleep, or the chemotherapy was inhibiting its normal functioning? A few weeks later, I boarded a plane and went visiting. I was depressed to meet her with an eerie glassy-fixated expression. She could hardly speak but mumbled some kind of pleasure at seeing me. I questioned her niece who was caring for her and learned that she had chemotherapy one week before my arrival. Within a couple of days, she deteriorated to the point that she needed help turning in bed. The following day, my dear friend was taken to the hospital for yet, another blood transfusion that was successful. The next day she no longer responded to any intervention. Her body was not having it anymore; more cells had broken down than had been built up. Her temple had endured one too many lethal bashings. My dear friend peacefully slipped into the abyss, we parted ways. She rests in peace.

People are scared to hear they have cancer because most people have experienced the brutal treatments and devastating effects of the dreadful disease in family, friends and acquaintances.

According to Jason Fung, in his book, 'The Cancer Code', "breast cancer cells thrive in the presence of insulin, and die when insulin is withdrawn". John Bergman, D.C further buttresses this point in a health video on YouTube saying, "Cancer is an adaptive metabolic process." We don't catch cancer, cancer is earned.

Maybe if she was privy to this information she would have done things differently and participated in her treatment. Who knows? She gorged on ice cream, drank malted beverages and ate whatever her heart desired, but did stay off red meat though.

According to Dr Colin T. Campbell, the author of 'The China Study' health is not derived from a pill instead health is derived from the "complex interactions with food."

The role of nutrition science and health is greatly ignored because it is much easier to pop a pill than to eat a whole food plant-based diet. However, for optimal health, proper nutrition is the key to wellness.

A visit to PubMed.gov revealed over one thousand studies on the role of a plant-based diet to reverse chronic diseases. Without a doubt, nutrition is the foundation of health.

https://www.youtube.com/watch?v=jD6TB_elbqg
https://www.youtube.com/watch?v=FlSRX6LWN-o

Ayurveda, traditional Indian medicine, puts it succinctly:

"If your food is wrong, medicine is of no use. If your food is right, medicine is of no need, Doctors don't make you healthy".

THE POWER OF NUTRITION

"At some point, you will have to realize only you are in charge of your destiny"

Dr Mindy Pelz

I recognize that there are various foods indigenous to all localities, but due to mono-cropping and issues of depleted soil, many nutrient-dense foods are swept into the abyss while we focus on cultivating and consuming a handful of crops. Proponents of whole food plant-based diets stress the need to include an array of colourful fruit and vegetable into our diets to access a wide range of vitamins, minerals, and phytonutrients.

In the light of whole food plant-based diet suggestions on how to maximize nutrient intake, I went digging and was pleasantly surprised to discover that there are many nutrient-dense foods indigenous to Africa that have been largely ignored. These nutrient-dense foods are not only for the benefit of Africans but for the global community at large since similar diseases ail us all regardless of our ancestral heritage. One of Chinua Achebe's quotes comes to mind:

"If you don't like someone's story, write your own"

To drive home my point, my granddaughter's paediatrician advised that we keep my thirteen-month-old Princess on cow milk formula and not feed her with our traditional African foods because it was constipating her. After a constant struggle with the parents to stop giving her lifeless food, I kept a food journal of what I fed her when she was with me. I took pictures of her rock-hard poop and sent them videos of her profuse sweating and distressing tears whenever she needed to move her bowels. Dogma is very hard to change, but it became evident that my granddaughter was unable to effectively digest the proteins in the cow milk formula. It never occurred to the paediatrician that my granddaughter could have been constipated because she was lactose intolerant. True to word, when her parents stopped giving her the formula and started feeding her with our indigenous meals of whole food plants, all her eczema cleared up, her wheezing ceased, the frequency of her bowel movements increased, and she is no longer distressed when she needs to move her bowels The fact remains, the traditional African diet is a whole food plant-based diet, a diet that has been scientifically proven to reverse chronic diseases and help maintain wellness. It is time that Africans remember the ancient landmarks, retrace their steps and return to their original diet in a bid to stay healthy and maintain wellness.

When growing up, for oral hygiene using a chewing stick was the norm. I often used chewing sticks as well; years later as a young adult, I visited a dentist in the USA to have a crown fixed. I was hit by a speeding motorbike when I was younger and the affected tooth was browning. The dentist complimented my teeth, saying, Africans have strong teeth. Twenty-eight years later, still, on the matter of the crown, I visited a dentist in the UK, and she said the same thing! As a young girl, I remember eating very little meat, feeding on plenty of fruits and vegetables in season. I particularly loved garden eggs, paw-paw, African walnuts, boiled groundnuts, and silky soft fufu wrapped in leaves. We planted jute leaves, okra and amaranth, and at harvest time my grandmother would prepare us freshly plucked jute leaf soup seasoned with fermented locust beans and fatty fish. It was so delicious that I always had to have a second helping of 'fufu' just to get more soup! The delightsome taste is still stuck in my memory. This is the power of food.

Many of us believe nutrition is ensuring we eat our starchy carbohydrates with plenty of animal protein at each meal. The more affluent the person; the more meat they can afford at each meal. Meanwhile, high consumption of meat is associated with a high risk for stroke, heart disease and diabetes. It is also linked to cancer. Most people eat three meat dishes daily, while some eat more than three meat dishes with a few meat snacks in between. Some people eat only cooked meals, and never eat fruits or vegetables. The variables differ, but the conclusion is that the above-mentioned diets will promote diseases.

On my journey to wellness, I watched food videos of Mark Weins who travels the world eating different dishes. I observed that human beings regardless of their race pretty much ate the same diet of starch and meat, however, most cultures add to their diet a wide variety of leaves and vegetables that are equally present in tropical Africa. Some of these leaves are cooked, and some of them are eaten raw. There are many plants that people who live in African cities are unaware of, nutrient-dense plants, which if added to their diets, would have a great impact on health outcomes.

For instance, in Thailand, raw cashew leaves are eaten with a rice dish; green paw-paw is made into a salad, similar to a popular salad dish, Abacha in the South-East of Nigeria. A simple mix of tomatoes, onions, and cucumber, mixed with lemon juice, Kachumbari, accompanies most dishes in East Africa.

Many people do not recognize that many plants contain protein, carbohydrates and fats; they believe that without animal protein a meal is not balanced. We do not recognize the importance of adding leafy greens to our diets and the role it plays in promoting good health. For instance, drinking vegetable juice could help lower blood pressure due to the potassium. Potassium helps relax blood vessels and reduce excess sodium in the cells. Fruits, vegetables, nuts and seeds are all forms of complex carbohydrates that supply the body with nutrients such as, magnesium, potassium, and phosphorous essential for the proper functioning of the body.

It is my mission that we create a movement that is focused on reversing diseases with nutrition. The real definition of a doctor means to teach, yet most doctors help their patients maintain sickness, instead of teaching them how to get well and maintain wellness. Whenever we feel dis-ease, a visit to the doctor's office is the first point of call. Hardly do we take the time to analyse our diets and make necessary changes. The doctor prescribes a pill to ameliorate the symptoms; once we start on the pill trajectory it becomes a vicious cycle.

Nutrition is more than macro-nutrients (carbohydrates, protein, and fat). It encompasses a broad array of vitamins, minerals and phytochemicals essential for health and for maintaining wellness. Vitamin and mineral deficiencies are known to cause diseases in the body. Examples of nutrient deficiencies are: Scurvy, a vitamin C deficiency, Beri-beri, a vitamin B1 deficiency, and Rickets in children are a vitamin D deficiency. Vitamin D deficiency is implicated in over 40 different ailments. I was astonished to learn that a vitamin B1 deficiency mimics diseases in five broad areas of health: cardiovascular/respiratory, digestion, autonomic nervous system/auto-immune disorders, neurons and the pancreas.

An example is POTS, a disorder where a person feels light-headed and faint when they arise from a sitting position, which is linked to a deficiency in vitamin B1. A vitamin B1 deficiency can also cause insomnia, a condition afflicting many people that is generally resolved by taking muscle relaxant prescription pills that come with side effects. If such a person is on medication this means they could be taking a pill for a disease that can be reversed by adding more nutrient-dense foods to their diet, or by supplementing with vitamin B1.

Falling asleep and maintaining sleep was a chronic issue for me until I changed my diet and lifestyle. On days that I didn't eat a proper meal, I would struggle to get four hours of sleep; and on days that I ate a diet of at least two servings of fruits and three to four servings of vegetables, I would sleep like a log. When I also added a pinch of salt to my water, I would sleep deeply. These days that I have added a variety of millets and vegetable juices to my diet, my sleep is deep and sweet. I bounce out of bed and turbo-charge throughout the day. My take is that if vitamin and mineral deficiencies can cause diseases, diseases can also be reversed with vitamins and minerals.

Most people still believe that using nutrition to treat diseases takes a long time, but I beg to differ. My personal experience has shown that if I feel joint pain during the day, and drink a turmeric latte as a nightcap, I awake not feeling the pain in my joints. Turmeric has been scientifically proven to be very effective at reducing inflammation. Moringa leaf powder is another plant that has helped me with joint pain.

In the 1950s, Dr Kempner designed a diet low in animal protein, and high in complex carbohydrates at Duke University. His diet, known as the 'rice diet' was shown to reverse end-stage kidney disease, hypertension and end-stage heart disease.

During my research, I was blown away by the number of people who had reversed chronic diseases with nutrition and lifestyle change. I was intrigued by Terry Wahls, MD who cured herself of Multiple Sclerosis, a debilitating chronic auto-immune disease, with food and lifestyle change. In the comments section of a YouTube video by John Campbell on vitamin D, I read the testimonial of a man who reversed Parkinson's disease by changing his diet and supplementing with vitamin D3 and K2. According to him, he had been committed to a nursing home because of his debilitating symptoms; and spent his days expecting death. His story changed when he signed up online for a course in nutrition. He learned about vitamin D and started taking it; when staff knew what he was doing they seized his stash because it was considered as self-medication. He sneakily continued taking a combination of vitamin D and K2; within six months he left the nursing home and can now take long hikes.

My excitement piqued when I read a testimonial in Joel Fuhrman's book, 'The End of Diabetes'. An 80-year-old woman who had been on insulin for 20 years was able to completely reverse type 2 diabetes. By eating a nutritious whole foods plant-based diet she was able to get off insulin in 10 days and discontinue all of her diabetes medication in one month. At the end of three months, her blood glucose readings were normal!

In William Li's book, 'Eat to Beat Disease', he lists foods that have been scientifically proven to turn on our health defences and help reverse diseases. He also wrote a personal testimonial of how his mother overcame cancer; she remains alive and prospering.

A 69-year-old woman recognized the power of nutrition when she presented to her doctor with aches, pains and stiffness in her joints (arthritis); she had high cholesterol and high blood pressure and was given a prescription. According to her, she was apprehensive about untimely death because most of her family members died from one disease or the other, and they lived most of their lives on prescription medicine, so she decided to change her diet. She added more fruit and vegetables, exercised and refused to take the medication. Within one week of a raw diet, all the arthritis was gone. She continued on her diet for six months till her next appointment. Her physician was glad to see that her blood pressure was as healthy as a young person's, and her cholesterol levels were normal. He commended the efficacy of the medication but was surprised to hear that she never took the medication. These testimonials attest to the power of nutrition.

I needed reading glasses by the time I was 39 years old and had more health issues to contend with once I turned 45 years. I suffered from alopecia, an auto-immune disorder; had borderline high blood pressure, high cholesterol, and tightness on the upper left side of my chest, stiff-achy fingers, and lower back pain and gall stones.

Before then, my diet had consisted of a daily dose of two freshly made jam doughnuts, a chocolate bar, four mugs of sweetened hot chocolate, beef or fish with every meal of starchy carbohydrates, and whatever my soul desired to consume. I also enjoyed a regular shot of brandy or a bottle of Guinness Stout.

I visited the doctor because my hair was falling out in large patches. After a round of blood tests to find the cause, I learned that I had high blood pressure, and was prescribed medication. The doctor referred me to a specialist when I refused to accept that I would have to take prescription medicine for the rest of my life. After a scan, I was informed that I had a bad case of gall stones. The specialist was surprised that I was not writhing in pain. I did feel discomfort on my lower back waist, but since I was used to popping aspirin, it was something that could be managed. He offered to do surgery to remove my gall bladder, but I politely declined since I had begun to glean knowledge about anatomy and physiology, nutrition and exercise from John Bergman, DC on YouTube.

I understood that the gall bladder is an important organ, essential for digestion, mineral absorption and wellness maintenance. I was able to learn how to expel gall stones with the oil treatment (oil treatment entails drinking one to two ounces of olive oil, chasing it down with a glass of warm water with a tablespoon of apple cider vinegar, and laying down on the right side for two hours) and how to keep my gall bladder stone-free by adding bile stimulating foods, such as beetroot, dandelion leaves, dandelion root tea, garlic and ginger to my diet. I still have my gallbladder intact and no longer experience lower-back pain. I was proactive; took responsibility for my health, and held on to my power to remain alive and healthy.

To tackle the high blood pressure, I started out taking the prescribed medication and going on half-hour walks. During my walks, a hill I used to be able to breeze through was becoming herculean to the point that I had to slow down and rest. Besides, the medication made my head feel like a heavy metal band concert. The headaches were clashing cymbals, and I hardly had headaches before this time. I complained to the doctor, and she dismissively asked me to continue on it till my body adjusted to the insidious assault.

I am usually introspective; maybe that could be a result of being a student of Philosophy, so taking a pill that was making my head pound and feel faint didn't make much sense to me. I was trying to get well and not get sicker. Then it dawned on me that I had to do something differently.

One of my books listed foods that could help naturally lower blood pressure, so I cleaned out my food cabinet to make room for health-promoting foods and hit the farmers market and grocery store. I added raw leafy greens to my diet, ate sardines, beets, raw cacao, fruits and vegetables, and brow-beat the chocolate bars, doughnuts, dairy, and sugary desserts, foods that were trying to cut short my precious boisterous life. I stopped by the health food store and bought supplements (chromium, and CoQ10); I also increased my walks to one hour five to six times weekly.

Another step I took was maintaining a food log, and twice-daily measured my blood pressure. I was expecting magic when it came to my blood pressure and was frustrated to read waking blood pressure at 145/96. I religiously stuck to my new diet and exercise program and noticed some difference in my systolic blood pressure reading on the third day. My waking blood pressure read 131/93; I did some deep breathing exercises (deep breathing exercises entails breathing through the nose, ensuring that the abdomen distends, and then slowly exhaling) and measured again, this time it read 129/92. It seemed like my little experiment was producing some results, even though my diastolic blood pressure seemed like it wouldn't budge. By day ten of changing my diet and lifestyle, my waking blood pressure read 115/83. All that was left for me to do was to stay on a diet of fruit and vegetables, and regular exercise. I was greatly encouraged to stay on track because I was able to shift my numbers within a short time without medication.

My food log the day prior:

Breakfast: A half-cup of Oatmeal with a tablespoon of chia seeds, butter croissant, a sautéed mix of bell peppers, celery, spinach and sardines, and one cup of chamomile tea.

Lunch: One cup of cherries and a 12-ounce cup of dark chocolate infused with turmeric beverage.

Dinner: Stir-fry noodles with peppers, cucumber and chicken.

Nightcap: 20ml of pomegranate juice.

According to John Bergman, D.C, in his YouTube video on blood pressure, a normal pulse pressure should be 40 points, which is subtracting the diastolic pressure from the systolic pressure. A pulse pressure above 40 points is an indication of underlying stressors, such as chemical, physical or emotional stress. Pulse pressure less than 40 is an indication that the heart is working hard because the blood isn't efficient. He recommends that we hydrate, and add more vegetable juice to our diets to aid in cleaning out the arteries because blood pressure is guided by our nutrition, and stress levels.

My doctor also prescribed me statins for high cholesterol. I went to fill out the prescription at the pharmacy and made to leave when the box of pills was handed to me. The attendant called me back for a repeat prescription; I was puzzled and asked her why I needed a repeat prescription after been handed a sixty-day supply. She told me high cholesterol was incurable, another life-sentence prescription. It was the most ridiculous thing I have ever heard that I never bothered to open the pack of pills.

I invested in another book titled '259 All-Natural Secrets to Disease-Proof Your Heart', a life-saving book chockfull of research-based natural remedies. The book recommended using Red Rice Yeast and Omega 3 supplements for high cholesterol, which I purchased and religiously consumed for 30 days. Afterwards, I took another cholesterol test and was happy to learn that my LDL cholesterol had gone down from 7.5 to 7. The cholesterol the pharmacy attendant said I had to be on drugs for, had budged. As a layperson, it was good news because it proved that my efforts made a difference in one month; I only had to stay on course and allow my body to restore itself to proper functioning.

Cholesterol is essential for the proper functioning of our brain, memory and hormones to the extent that when it is too low, serotonin cannot effectively perform its function. Serotonin is known as the feel-good chemical, which means that people with low levels of cholesterol may be at risk for depression. High cholesterol is an indication of some damage in the arteries.

I know we have always been told to follow our physician's recommendations, but what if the physician refuses to acknowledge my concerns? Doctors are supposed to teach us how to get back to wellness, but do they? We all know the answer to that question. It didn't, and still doesn't make sense to me that I have to be on medication for the rest of my life to stay alive. I reasoned that staying on medication for life simply meant perpetual ill health, and my goal was to stay alive in wellness. My physician didn't share my goals so we had to part ways. Can two people remain friends without a common goal?

Without health there's no freedom; health is our natural state. You are tethered to the apron strings of the pharmaceutical industry if you don't participate in your treatment.

In the words of Joel Fuhrman, M.D, "You can't drug yourself into good health"

Even though sceptics still exist in the face of these glaring changes, there is enough anecdotal evidence available to prove that it is possible and more effective to reverse disease with diet instead of chugging a handful of pills. It is wiser to work with a nutritionist, naturopath, chiropractor, or some other natural health practitioner to get well and work with a doctor when there is a crisis.

Nutrition dives to the foundation of the problem to uproot the disease because it fills the gap of deficiencies, plugs the drain of leeching nutrients, and floods the body with antioxidants to help flush out harmful substances obstructing the path to restoration and regeneration. Life begets life, and by eating live foods with enzymes we provide the body with the fuel it needs to effectively repair, restore, and rejuvenate damaged cells.

Since eating is something we all have to do anyway why not make the best of this essential process by eliminating disease-causing foods, and adding health-promoting foods to our diets?

KEYS TO HEALTH

> *"Muscle and joint discomforts are common signs your body isn't working the way it's supposed to. Nutrient deficiencies can prevent healthy hormone levels and a normal immune system."*
>
> Eric Berg, DC

Baby steps in the right direction will yield great results when it comes to our health. As we get older we produce less stomach acid and cannot easily digest proteins into amino acids, and fat into fatty acids, which is why it is advisable to eat according to our energy needs. Eating less meat and increasing our vegetable intake; juicing and eating fermented foods are ways to keep our bodies functioning at full capacity.

Most of my friends and family on one pill or the other would complain about the drudgery of chugging a handful of oblong, round and oval shapes in different colours. A few of them have abruptly stopped taking their medication and have ended up on a hospital bed. The problem is that many people do not know how to take control of their health with nutrition, and keep wolfing down foods that got them on medication in the first place. They want to use food as medicine to reverse their diseases, but they don't know what to eat, neither do they truly understand the healing power of food.

According to William Li, MD the author of 'Eat to Beat Disease', "Food is better than medication to treat disease"

Throughout my research and journey to wellness, I noted a common thread on the first rung of the disease-reversal and wellness maintenance ladder. There are seven major steps to health:

1. Sleep: it is suggested we sleep for a minimum of seven hours, which should amount to five 90-minute cycles of REM sleep. During deep sleep, damaged cells are rejuvenated, restored and begin to function properly. This is why we should allow all digestion to take place before bedtime. It is not surprising that many cancers are linked to a lack of adequate sleep.

    Also, when we don't sleep well, we are unable to adequately produce hydrochloric acid that is essential for the digestion of food and extraction of nutrients from food.

Sleep was an area where I struggled for many years, needing to drink coffee for that essential boost of energy during the day. Wherever I globe-trotted, I lugged around my coffee percolator, and a bag of ground roasted coffee. Even though I still drink coffee, it is limited to one 12-ounce cup three to four times weekly.

TIPS: Some days, I drink Chamomile tea throughout the day and on other days, I drink celery juice. I also eat bananas (organic), boil the peels and add a pinch of nutmeg. Potassium and magnesium are essential nutrients for sleep so it is advisable to consume plants rich in magnesium. Leafy greens, raw cacao powder, blackstrap molasses, and grains are some rich magnesium foods. For best results, cacao can be consumed during the day because it contains caffeine that might interfere with sleep. Not eating enough food or the right kinds of foods during the day can also affect sleep; therefore it is wise to monitor your food intake to avoid the vicious cycle of nutrient deficiency and disease.

2. Exercise, Prayer and Meditation: walking, high-intensity interval training, swimming, and weight lifting. Prayer walks and speaking affirmative words also have great healing effects. Exercise is recommended because it oxygenates the body and prevents our arteries from clogging up.

    TIPS: It is safe to start the exercise with 15-minute walks, and gradually increase. I love taking sixty to ninety-minute walks, five times weekly. Walking helps clear my head and aids my thinking process. On walks, I also pray, meditate, and mull over pressing issues.

3. Sunlight/Fresh air: research has shown a link between low and sub-optimal levels of vitamin D in the blood and many diseases. A doctor in the USA reported treating patients with various disorders, ranging from infertility to depression with vitamin D supplementation. She reported amazing results and advised that we should check our vitamin D levels to ensure optimal blood levels.

    When I had issues with high blood pressure, I sunbathed between forty-five minutes and one hour, took a shower and measured my blood pressure. To my amazement, my readings constantly fell within normal ranges, however, when I took my blood pressure reading before bed, it would show the fearsome numbers that I hated to see. It simply shows that sunlight is indeed medicine.

TIPS: if you live in a warm climate, sunbathe in the morning, exposing as many parts as possible to allow the sun to do its magic. For light-skinned people, 30-40 minutes of sunlight exposure is recommended. For dark-skinned people, 45 minutes to one hour is recommended. In more temperate climes, it is best to supplement with vitamin D3. Please consult with your physician for testing and recommended dose.

4. Intermittent fasting: eating within a 'window' of time will help maintain healthy insulin levels in the blood. To keep it simple, skipping breakfast, or dinner will give the body time to rest. The rule; however is that all meals must be consumed within eight hours for men and within a ten-hour window for women.

   Intermittent fasting is important because of the hormone, insulin. Insulin metabolizes carbohydrates, removing glucose from the blood and transporting it into the cells, and storing it as glycogen, while the rest is stored as fat. Our cells are small and can only take so much, thus when it is full it resists the onslaught of more glucose. This condition is known as insulin resistance where insulin receptors don't work properly. When this happens, it is difficult to maintain a healthy body weight, which precipitates illness. High glucose levels in the blood is implicated in diseases such as type-2 diabetes, kidney diseases and high blood pressure, just to mention a few.

Foods that spike insulin are: processed foods without fibre, trans-fat, sugar, baked goods, a combination of starchy vegetables and animal protein.

I have since adopted a fasting lifestyle, and do intermittent fasting for 16-18 hours on most days, though it is recommended that women fast for 14-16 hours. According to Mindy Pelz, MD the body goes through a process called autophagy, a detoxifying process when fasting periods hit 18 hours.

TIPS: Mindy Pelz recommends intermittent fasting five days weekly, one day of a 24-hour fast, and one day of re-fuelling the body with nutrient-dense foods. The best way to rid the body of metabolic waste is fasting. My weight has since dropped from 66 kilograms; hovers between 55-56 kilograms.

5. Wholefood Plant-based diet: many nutritionists encourage a plant-based diet to provide the body with nutrients essential for growth and development, and to provide the body with fibre essential for our gastrointestinal health. We know about vitamins and minerals, but recent developments have shown that plants have phytonutrients that provide antioxidants necessary to reverse diseases caused by metabolic waste, free radicals and environmental toxins; and to maintain wellness.

   Before adopting a whole foods diet, I used to have irregular bowel movements. Being clogged up for five days was no big deal, and didn't stop me from further stuffing down more food. My mid-section stretched to accommodate the contents, but that changed when daily, I started drinking Moringa herbal tea.

TIPS: I have since added more fibre to my diet in the form of African wild rice, finger and pearl millet, yams and loads of leafy greens. These days, once to twice daily, depending on how often I eat, my bowels move without the aid of laxatives.

6. Emotional Health: it is equally important to maintain a grudge-free mind because ill feelings build up toxins in the body. Talk to a trusted person when you have emotional issues, and learn the art of forgiveness. It has been proven that emotions play a role in the development of cancer.

    In the past, I was a master-grudger. I could unflinchingly hold a grudge for years; however, my life positively blossomed when I invested in a book, "Anger is a Choice", by Tim LaHaye and Bob Phillips. I now understand the principle of forgiveness and the art of communication.

    TIPS: I speak my mind, ask questions and try not to assume anything. I always remember the words of a dear friend, "Always give people the benefit of doubt". This is my new mantra so much that I forgave my cousin who sexually abused me as a child, and forgave my cousin who physically abused me before he passed away.

7. Digestive health: it is important for optimal functioning of the immune system since everything we eat is processed in the gut. It is purported that 80% of our immune system is in our gastrointestinal tract where nutrients essential for health is extracted from ingested food. Therefore, for good digestive health, it is advisable to eat fermented foods, and drink water. Staying hydrated is important to keep things moving as expected.

To adequately prepare the body for nutrient extraction, it is important to note the following useful tips:

(a) Always start your day with lemon and warm water, or a tablespoon of ACV in a glass of warm water, or a cup of bitter herbs. Drinking this first thing in the morning helps to stimulate bile, alkalizing the body and preparing it for meals. This will also help facilitate bowel movements essential to keep the body clean from waste.

(b) Cut out processed foods, and sugar. Sugar is said to cause metabolic sludge, raise insulin levels and blood fat.

I made the mistake of not reading the back label on a carton of coconut water that had ninety-nine% boldly printed on it. I first noted some discomfort around my waistline, especially when seated, so I weighed myself and was aghast to see that I had gained two kilograms despite fasting daily. I also began to have searing pain in my waist that I needed help rising up from a seated position. Even if I wanted to see a doctor, it was impossible due to the pandemic and lockdown. This was a period that proved great gains from all the years of learning about how the body functions. To get to the root of the problem, I laid flat on my back and applied pressure to different points on my abdomen. I observed that applying pressure on the site of my gallbladder sent searing pain to the left side of my lower back. I figured that it could be a case of gallstones.

Weeks later, while in a conversation with my son about the price of coconut water, I discovered that the brand I had been consuming had fructose in it, even though it had ninety-nine % blazoned on the carton.

As soon as I cut out the fructose, and flushed my gallbladder with olive oil, the pain subsided. I finished off the cleanse by drinking vegetable juice made from a combination of celery, cavolo nero, dandelion greens, bitter melon and ginger. In a few days, I was up and running as if nothing had happened.

(c) Eat fermented foods daily such as peanut yoghurt and fermented vegetables. It is essential for health because a change in the colony of our gut microbiome causes a myriad of diseases. These bacteria, yeasts and fungi help the body produce nutrients, such as short-chain fatty acids.

Our microbiome is affected by dietary factors and the use of antibiotics, so it is important to daily repopulate our gut with healthy bacteria found in fermented foods. Remarkable results have been reported transferring microbes from the faeces of healthy people to the gut of sick people to help them get well.

TIPS: I make fermented hibiscus tea, or fermented beetroot juice a part of my meals instead of drinking fruit juice loaded with sugar. It also aids digestion. (I give the juice to my granddaughter as it helps with constipation and compacted stool.)

(d) Chew food thoroughly to aid digestion. I am still a work in progress when it comes to chewing my food. I try to be more conscious, especially when I eat a meal with mucilage soup.

(e) Eating mono-meals helps the body better digest food. An example of mono-meals is eating animal protein with non-starchy vegetables, and eating starchy carbohydrates with leafy greens. Digested food means better vitamin and mineral absorption. I try to eat animal protein with less starchy vegetables like cabbage, leafy greens, broccoli and so on; and eat starchy grains and vegetables with leafy greens, okra, egusi, and so on.

TIPS: on days that I plan to eat animal protein, I ensure that I add a serving of pineapple, or kiwi fruit, or paw-paw (papaya) to my breakfast meal. These fruits are known for their digestive enzyme properties that will aid the digestion and absorption of protein. Animal protein is the last thing anyone should have lingering in their digestive tract as it is implicated in the onset of diet-related cancers, such as breast, colon, and prostate cancers.

(f) Drink water regularly adding a pinch of Celtic or pink salt. It is essential for cellular hydration and to keep the kidneys from developing stones.

TIPS: to make drinking water palatable, I squeeze in some lemon, or lime juice, and add a pinch of pink Himalayan salt.

Following the above tips has improved my health in leaps and bounds. My bodyweight has remained stable. I receive regular compliments about my skin, my joints are supple, and my energy has increased. I feel more energetic than I did when I was in my twenties.

NUTRIENT-RICH AFRICAN CROPS/FOODS

> *"Africa's own edibles have yet to receive due attention, let alone a chance to develop to their potential... Science tends to beam its searchlight on crops that can garner cash, like soybean, while Africa's yam and okra are left in the shadows"*
>
> 'Lost Crops of Africa'

There are many foods indigenous to Africans that have been lost in the maze of imported foods and crops. The modern way of farming has limited our food choices and swept our nutritious indigenous crops under the carpet of big corporations. This means that our access to nutrient intake is limited; we are unable to benefit from a wide variety of crops that could provide our cells with the life-giving vitamins, minerals and phytochemicals that abounds in those crops/plants.

For instance, most African countries have as staples corn (maize) and cassava, to the exclusion of more nutritious grains and tubers.

In the book, 'The Lost Crops of Africa', the authors claim that "the diets of many African communities are deficient in vitamins, minerals and other nutrients." This does not make much sense because we have available nutrient-dense crops that have been ignored, excluded from mainstream diets.

I have personally heard Africans disparage indigenous meals, and would rather eat couscous made from wheat because they believe it is better. On the contrary, many unrecognized indigenous nutrient-dense grains and seeds pack a nutritious punch above Wheat. Some Africans would rather opt for aquaponic spinach, rather than buy amaranth grown in mineral-rich soil, which is not to say that aquaponic spinach is inedible, but to show that we should not disparage traditional vegetables.

Below, are some of our indigenous crops and vegetables that are more nutritious than wheat, corn and spinach. Wherever you live on the globe these foods are available. If you live in the diaspora you can buy these foods from your local Asian (Indian, Sri-Lankan, Pakistani, Thai) grocery shops.

All information about our indigenous crops and plants were culled from the books, 'The Lost Crops of Africa', Volumes I, II, and III, except for the information on African oil palm. I have listed a few with their nutrient profiles so that you can understand how valuable they are. For more information, a Google search will provide more details.

GRAINS

African rice (Oryza glaberrima): its nutritional quality is said to be greater than Asian rice. It is more difficult to polish, which means it can retain most of its nutrients. African rice, "in some vitamins and mineral, it is far superior". It contains *thiamine*, a great source of vitamin B1. This rice can be found in Asian grocery shops as 'village rice'. Red unpolished rice is also a good substitute.

Finger Millet (Eleusine corocana): is said to be "one of the most nutritious" of all major cereals because of its high level of *methionine*, an amino acid that is lacking in the diet of people who live on starchy foods. Finger millet contains up to 61% of total digestible nutrients. It is high in calcium, magnesium, phosphorus and potassium. Please note that milk is not the only source of calcium. What makes this cereal a great food source is that it is high in protein and amino acids essential to human health and growth. This grain is available in Asian shops as 'Ragi'. It is available as a whole grain or milled as flour.

Fonio/Acha/Hungry Rice (Digitaria Iburua, Digitaria exilis): this cereal crop is said to be a better alternative to Couscous that is derived from wheat. It contains twice as much *methionine* as an egg. This means that it is possible to get more nutrients from this cereal than from the eggs of caged birds. This grain is available locally in most African countries and can be purchased online if you live in the diaspora. Foxtail millet is a good substitute that can be purchased from Asian shops.

Pearl Millet (Pennistum glaucum): this is a recommended cereal for diabetics due to its low glycemic load. It contains two-thirds insoluble fibre, and between 9-21 % proteins depending on the soil it is grown in. It also contains 5 % fat, 5-7 % oil; rich in vitamin A, magnesium, iron, folate, phosphorus, B-vitamins, calcium and amino acids. It is "nutritionally superior" to wheat, rice, maize and sorghum. This grain is called 'Bajri' in Asian shops available as whole grains or milled as flour.

Sorghum (Sunlight Plant): there are many varieties of this grain that are used as animal feed, and for human consumption. The main problem is that it contains tannis, which are indigestible proteins. In Africa, our ancestors learned to dominate their environment and extract whatever was necessary for health and wellness; that is why we have a culture of fermenting foods before consumption. Sorghum is fermented for 7-10 days before it is milled. It contains potassium and phosphorus; high levels of B-vitamins and *tryptophan* than maize, and is a good source of "more than 20 micro-nutrients". This grain is available as 'Jowar' in Asian shops.

Tef (Eragrostis tef): this is a staple in Ethiopia, used to make Injera bread. It is fast gaining popularity across the world because of its nutrient profile. It contains a good level of minerals, "rich in iron, calcium, potassium, and phosphorus". The iron levels are said to be higher than those of wheat, barley and sorghum; and also contains an "excellent balance of essential amino acids". This grain can easily be purchased online.

Judging from the above, it is possible to maintain a healthy diet without gorging on animal protein.

VEGETABLES

Amaranth (Amaranthus): a leafy green vegetable that also produces seeds that can be used as a grain. It contains iron, calcium, vitamins A and C. It also contains about 30 % protein in the leaves. It is high in *lysine*, an amino acid found in eggs. This leafy green is available in Asian, African, and Caribbean grocery shops.

Bambara Beans/Nuts (Vigna subterranea): is a "complete food" that contains 60 % carbohydrates, 20% protein, and 6 % oil. It is high in *methionine* compared to other grains and legumes. This true groundnut can be purchased online, or in African speciality grocery shops.

Baobab (Adansonia digitata linnaeus): the leaf contains proteins, vitamins and minerals. It is high in *lysine and tryptophan.* The fruit is particularly high in vitamin C. This prized plant is mostly available locally, but the powdery fruit can be purchased online and added to smoothies. Some chefs also use it to season fish because of its lime-like flavour.

Celosia (Celosia argentea): is a leafy green vegetable that is high in calcium, phosphorus, iron and vitamins. It contains a "considerable amount of protein". It is popularly called, 'Soko' in the Yoruba dialect.

Cowpea (Vigna unguiculata): it contains 24% nutritional protein that is "free of suppressing metabolites" that is available in soybeans. It is high in *lysine*. This legume is nitrogen-fixing to the soil that boosts the yield of cereal grains when grown in rotation. This is available in most grocery shops. It is commonly known as 'Black-eyed peas'. Other varieties of cowpeas are available in African shops.

Dika Nut (Irvingia gabonenesis): this nut is high in oil and protein. "60 % oil, 30 % carbohydrates, 8% protein". It contains six essential amino acids. The bright orange-coloured fruit is consumed for the nut, however, the outer flesh is high in vitamin A and has more vitamin C than pineapple or orange. This is available in African shops, commonly known as 'Ogbonno'.

Garden egg (Solanum aethiopicum): is great for weight watchers because it is high in potassium and dietary fibre. It is usually enjoyed with peanut butter (spicy-roasted milled groundnut paste). This is a variety of eggplant (aubergine) and is available for purchase at African shops. Aubergine is a good substitute.

Egusi (Citrullus lanatus): is the seed of a melon high in nutrients, a great vegetable protein. It contains more than 50 % oil and 30% protein; "an excellent source of *arganine, methionine, tryptophan and niacin*; vitamin B1 and 2". This super-seed also contains potassium, magnesium, sulphur, calcium, iron and zinc. This precious seed can be purchased from most African shops, it is also available at Asian shops as, 'Charmagaz'.

Lablab (Lablab purpureus): is a legume with a 20-28 %protein; "amino acids are moderately well balanced". It is high in *lysine*, but contains anti-nutrient factors like soybeans. Fermentation will make available the nutrients in this plant. The leaves are also rich in protein and iron. This legume can be purchased at Asian shops.

Locust Bean (Parkia biglobosa): is made up of 7% protein, a level "similar to that in a whole egg". It also contains vitamins; high in linoleic fatty acids, and fibre. Locust beans are usually fermented and added to soups as a seasoning. This popular condiment is available online and in African shops, it can be purchased in dehydrated or wet forms.

Moringa (Moringa oleifera): every part of this plant packs a nutritional punch. The pods contain all the essential amino acids, vitamins A, B, and C. It is also filled with minerals like iron and calcium. The leaves contain *methionine* and *cystein*. This African superfood has gained the limelight and is available in most health food stores.

Okra (Abelmoschus esculentus): this is an equally exceptional vegetable because the pods, seeds and leaves have dietary value. Half a cup of the cooked pods provides the body with 10% of the daily recommended levels of vitamin B6 and folate. (Remember the town in Nigeria with a 95% rate of twins? The okra plant and yam, a root crop is the staple diet) Okra has fair amounts of vitamins A and C. The seeds are rich in ***tryptophan*** and sulphur. The protein in okra "complements many cereal grains, legumes and root crops. This nutritious crop is available in most African/Caribbean and Asian grocery shops.

Yambean (Sphenostylis stenocarpa): this plant provides food from the seeds and roots. The seeds are 1/4 protein with amino acids similar to that of the soybean. The roots, tubers, are very nutritious and contain about 10-20 % protein. This is mostly available on the continent. If you live outside Africa, enjoy it when you visit home.

FRUIT

Butter fruit (Dacryodes edulis): commonly known as African pear. The pulp is 33-65 % rich in oil and is a rich source of protein (20-30 %). The fruit is high in **lysine** and **tryptophan**, and also contains potassium, calcium, magnesium, iron zinc and copper. It is mostly enjoyed with roasted corn. "...the levels of lysine leucine and threonine are similar to those found in top-quality animal proteins... and much higher than those in most plant staple foods such as wheat, barley, rye, rice maize, sorghum or melon seeds". This nutritious fruit can be purchased from African speciality stores when in season.

Tamarind (Tamarind indica): is a good source of **thiamine, niacin,** and **riboflavin**. It also contains some iron but is rich in phosphorus, potassium, and calcium. These minerals are in higher amounts in the tamarind, compared to any other fruit. The proteins are also high in essential amino acids. This fruit has gained ground and is cultivated in many Asian countries. Thailand is a big producer, and it is available year-round in Asian grocery shops. It can be purchased de-seeded, or as a whole fruit.

African oil Palm (Elaesis guineensis): is a good source of vitamin E, antioxidants, and beta carotene, a precursor to vitamin A. "Red palm oil has been calculated to have 15 times more of these health-giving carotenes than carrots and 300 times more than tomatoes". The vitamin E present in palm oil has both ***tocopherol*** and ***tocotrienols***. "The antioxidant effect of the tocotrienols can not only prevent cancer but can also help to kill off cancer cells." Red palm oil has been shown to lessen the effects of strokes because it can prevent neurological degeneration. It is also beneficial in lowering cholesterol levels, maintaining healthy blood pressure, and strengthening the heart. The whole nut can be seasonally purchased from African speciality shops, and the oil or cream is available all year in African/Caribbean grocery shops.

Honourable Mention

Snails have anti-inflammatory properties and contain essential fatty acids, calcium, iron, selenium, magnesium; they are also rich in vitamins A, E, K, and vitamin B12. Snails are a great addition to the diet to replace red meat, especially factory-farmed meat.

Sugarcane is rich in iron, calcium and magnesium. Even though it is sweet, it is a great addition to a plant-based diet because of the nutrient profile.

Nutrient Profiles: Vitamins, Minerals and Amino-acids

I listed above some indigenous foods of Africa with their nutrient profiles; to show that nutrients are essential for our wellness, below I'll simplify some functions, deficiencies and food sources of the vitamins, minerals and amino-acids (protein building blocks). Many foods contain carbohydrates, proteins, and fat in varying amounts, so most foods will contain a combination of B-vitamins, amino acids, and fats.

Thiamine is a B-vitamin that helps our body turn food into energy. It keeps the nervous system healthy and is involved in five different enzymes in the body. This B-vitamin protects the cells from oxidation and from becoming sticky; especially important to prevent damage to nerves and complications from high blood sugar.

Deficiencies include, but not limited to the following:

1. Cardiovascular and respiratory diseases.
2. Digestive issues: constipation, low hydrochloric acid, sluggish digestion.
3. Neuropathy, vertigo, neuritis.
4. Auto-immune disorders.

5. Insomnia, brain fog, anxiety, tension, sleep apnea, dizziness with rising from a seated position.
6. Problems with the pancreas, such as pancreatic cancer.

Food Sources: African rice, pearl millet, sorghum, cowpea, egusi, dika nut, tamarind, oranges and liver.

Methionine and Cystein are amino acids essential in the repair of the body because they are the building blocks of protein. Glutathionine is known as the body's natural antioxidant that keeps us from premature ageing, protects our DNA from damage and repairing damaged cells. Methionine and cystein work synergistically, aiding the body to produce glutathionine.

Deficiencies include, but not limited to the following:

1. Premature ageing
2. Replication of cancerous cells
3. Heart disease

Food Sources: sulphur rich foods, Moringa plant, finger millet, fonio, bambara nuts, egusi and mushrooms.

Zinc is a trace mineral that acts as a co-factor in over one thousand enzymes. It is essential for the proper functioning of the immune system and is important for skin structure and the liver.

Deficiencies include, but not limited to the following:
1. Respiratory infections
2. Skin and hair disorders
3. Retarded growth
4. Insulin production
5. Ulcers
6. Macular degeneration
7. Prostate issues
8. Depression
9. Inflammation
10. Mood disorders
11. Nerve degeneration
12. Low testosterone. Sperm is rich in zinc and a deficiency affects its production.

Food Sources: Egusi, cacao powder, sorghum, sesame seeds, bambara nut, avocado, tigernuts, guava, garlic, amaranth, mushrooms, butterfruit, okra.

Arganine is another amino acid that plays a role in blood vessel dilation by relaxing the arteries. It also helps with immune system function and aids the body in the removal of ammonia that can be toxic to the kidneys. The downside of this amino acid is that if you suffer bouts of herpes, consuming too much of it may exacerbate the problem. Adding vitamin C foods to the diet might help to ameliorate this problem.

Deficiencies include, but not limited to the following:

1. Low blood flow to the brain and lungs
2. High free radicals causing inflammation in the body.
3. Erectile dysfunction
4. High LDL cholesterol
5. Kidney disease
6. Slow wound healing

Food Sources: African rice, cashew, groundnuts, egusi, pearl millet, dika nut, butterfruit.

Magnesium is another important mineral that has over five hundred functions in the body. It helps the body in absorbing and breaking down other minerals and vitamins.

Deficiencies include, but not limited to the following:

1. Leg cramps and foot aches
2. Gum aches
3. Fatigue
4. Insomnia
5. Muscle weakness, or stiffness.

Food Sources: Amaranth, cacao powder, sugar cane, finger millet, pearl millet, dika nut.

Lysine is an amino-acid that aids in the absorption of calcium, and collagen production. It also helps with viral infections. A synergy of Lysine and Methionine produces Carnitine, which protects against cardio-vascular disease, chronic fatigue, high triglycerides, leg cramps, male infertility and age-related cognitive impairment.

Deficiencies include, but not limited to the following:

1. Bodyweight issues
2. Sagging skin
3. Cold sores
4. Anxiety disorder
5. Achy joints
6. Slow wound healing

Food Sources: Lablab, amaranth, baobab leaf, moringa leaf, butterfruit, avocado, cowpea, eggs, red meat.

Niacin is a B-vitamin essential for the optimal functioning of the body. It helps with a healthy nervous system, aids digestive health and good skin. It equally helps lower LDL cholesterol.

Deficiencies include, but not limited to the following:

1. Problems with memory (mental confusion)
2. Fatigue
3. Skin problems (pellagra)
4. Headaches
5. Behaviour problems
6. Headaches
7. Cracked heels

Food Sources: Tamarind, groundnuts, avocado, mushrooms, native potatoes, yambean, beef and chicken liver, cowpeas.

Tryptophan is an amino acid which when combined with B-vitamins helps the body produce serotonin. Serotonin is known as the feel-good chemical that is essential for mental health, appetite, sleep and pain.

Deficiencies include, but not limited to the following:

1. Mood disorders
2. Memory problems
3. Motion sickness
4. Premenstrual symptoms
5. Impulsive behaviour
6. Insomnia

Food Sources: Okra, sorghum, baobab, egusi, butterfruit.

Vitamin E (Tocotrienols and tocophernols) are antioxidants that protect our cells from chemical/free radical damage. It is a fat-soluble vitamin that is essential for the proper functioning of the immune system. It is also regarded by some as an aphrodisiac because it helps with blood circulation.

Deficiencies include, but are not limited to the following:

1. Weak immune system
2. Nerve damage
3. Low libido
4. Vision problems.
5. Hair loss

Food Sources: Red palm nut cream/oil, groundnuts, egusi, leafy greens.

PRESSING ISSUES: WHAT'S NEXT?

"Health and life span can be extended by packing in more micronutrient diversity"

Joel Fuhrman, M.D

On the journey to wellness, several steps need to be taken to ensure that nutrition works effectively. It is not only essential to eliminate toxic food and skincare products; it is also important that we prepare our minds for healing by tending to our emotional health. Emotional health is an area often ignored. We seek to heal our bodies when symptoms arise but never seek to resolve our pressing negative emotional issues capable of seeping toxins into our bodies.

After addressing chemical, emotional and physical toxins only then is it time to add life-giving nutrients to our diets by eating a varied range of fruits, vegetables and whole grains. Most diets focus on what to eliminate, which is an important part of the equation, but when a diet demands eliminating antioxidant-rich fruits from the diet, it further limits choices and variety.

As Africans, we tend to only eliminate what is inedible, which makes it a diet focused on flooding the body with nutrients essential for healing and wellness. Not only do we not eliminate foods, but we also tend to add herbs to the mix, especially when we are trying to get well.

According to Eric Berg, a Ketogenic diet and wellness expert, people with weight issues should never be focused on losing weight, instead, he advises that they should be focused on getting well, and the weight will drop off as the body gets healthy. His position suggests that obesity is a part of the sum and not a sum in itself. It is a general health issue, and not merely a single weight issue.

Obesity, weight issues, makes us susceptible to many diseases, including cancer. Jason Fung, in the 'Cancer Code', lists a variety of cancers associated with overweight, and obesity, "... ovary, colon and rectum, pancreas, upper stomach, gall bladder, liver, breast and thyroid"

All diet types focus on helping the user maintain healthy body weight, however, maintaining a healthy body weight does not necessarily translate to being adequately nourished. For this main reason, I agree with the school of whole foods plant-based because it simplifies eating without the stress of eliminating tasty vitamin-mineral filled foods; it is more focused on flooding the body with life-giving nutrients. Whole foods plant-based is not overly focused on what to exclude from the diet; instead, it beams the floodlight on what we benefit from eating all plants regardless of their carbohydrate or sugar content. I don't need to eliminate many foods and substitute those foods with supplements. For instance, a Ketogenic diet expert denounces the eating of fruit but advises the use of electrolyte powder to avoid the sugar in fruit. A piece of fruit does have sugar, but it also contains fibre, vitamins and minerals.

I adhered to the African whole foods plant-based diet, followed basic food combination principles, and unintentionally lost weight even though my goal was to quell inflammation in my body.

During my food to wellness experiment, I planned my meals according to Dr Joel Fuhrman's Nutritarian diet in his book, 'The End of Diabetes'. A diet he defines as, "an eating style in which the vast majority of calories are obtained from eating natural, colourful, nutrient-rich plant foods". I partially followed his dietary recommendations since I didn't eat much fruit, but ate very little animal protein, about five ounces weekly; continued with my exercise program of walking for an hour five to six times weekly. I also did 16-hour intermittent fasts six times weekly. At the end of one year, family and friends complained about my weight loss; colleagues at work thought I had cancer because I was skinny. I dropped from 62 kilograms to 51 kilograms.

I believe the diet worked due to an emphasis on eating whole foods, despite the 'low-carb' hype since all I ate were carbohydrates: beans prepared in different ways. My goal for trying out the diet was to grow back my hair, but I unintentionally lost weight. The mistake I made was in not ingesting enough calories daily so my hair issues were not resolved as expected.

In conclusion, Dr Fuhrman's recommended eating plan worked as intended; a success in helping with weight loss and in reversing diabetes. Understanding how your metabolism works is important to help you stay healthy.

I now eat according to my caloric needs, keep animal protein at 0.4 grams per kilogram of body weight per meal a minimum of thrice weekly, and a maximum of four times weekly. I hardly combine animal protein with my starchy vegetables like yam and have since added more leafy greens to my diet. I combine my greens with animal protein, which enhances the absorption of nutrients because leafy greens are mostly fat-soluble.

Standing at five feet six inches tall, my weight has been comfortably stable at 56 kilograms, and my hair has started to sprout on some areas of my glossy bald patches albeit slowly, nevertheless an accomplishment after almost twelve years of my scalp looking like Swiss cheese.

HOME REMEDIES

When diseases occur, it is common to see that people get worried when doctors are unable to reach a diagnosis as if the diagnosis is the treatment. I often ask, after diagnosis then what? Nine out of ten times the answer to my question is a blank stare. I lost a dear friend to cancer, which has prompted this section of the discussion. When she was feeling symptoms, for months she made the rounds to the hospital to no avail. At some point, doctors thought she was hypochondriac, but her symptoms were real. Many tests had been done, but nothing showed up that could explain her symptoms.

She presented with acute backaches and was prescribed opioids for the debilitating pain. I suggested regular use of turmeric with black pepper, hoping that whatever was causing the inflammation would be tamed. I reasoned that there could be a growing tumour pressing on some nerve, which was causing the excruciating pain. I also suggested using a probiotic because I had learned that our microbiome works to keep us healthy, and a regular dose of antibiotics in her treatment protocol would probably have wiped out her friendly colony.

I strongly believe that while we await that doctor's appointment or a diagnosis, it is wise to do something in the interim. It is better than sitting around twiddling our thumbs waiting for a miracle. The seemingly inconsequential things we do could be the miracle we are expecting. Diagnosis aids treatment, but it is not treatment in itself. My friend regularly visited the hospital for over three months and used the prescribed pain medication while she awaited a diagnosis so that treatment could commence, by the time doctors were able to figure out the problem, it was already too late. The main focus was on relieving the pain, anything to manage the excruciating pain; I don't blame her, excruciating pain would drive anyone insane.

At the first sign of symptoms, no matter how small, it is important to define our health goals. Do you want to manage the disease, or you want to uproot the disease? Never ignore the smallest symptom in your body. Defining your health goals will determine your course of action.

For instance, my friend had been complaining of back pains for as long as I can remember, but when symptoms arose she was quick to reach for the 'painkiller broom to sweep symptoms under the carpet. The wisest decision anyone can make regarding health: never ignore symptoms regardless of how minute.

There is a great fear of chronic diseases, especially cancer because of the feelings of hopelessness it conveys; nevertheless, we are not helpless. According to Jason Fung, in his book, 'The Cancer Code', "cancer requires decades to develop". His position might sound implausible in the face of childhood cancers, but makes plenty of sense in adult cancers. You can start now by following a nutrient-rich diet that will enable your body to shed excess weight that could put you at risk for debilitating diseases. Obesity is a certain precursor to diseases.

For instance, I listened to the testimony of a woman who was given a death sentence but remains alive and well 19 years later to tell her story. She was diagnosed with incurable breast cancer and started drinking 8-12 cups of vegetable juice daily.

There are simple home remedies you can do while you await that doctor's appointment or diagnosis.

THE POWER OF TURMERIC

Turmeric and black pepper have been scientifically proven to help with inflammation, and pain relief. It is useful in breast, colon and pancreatic cancer. A visit to PubMed reveals over 1,700 research papers on the effects of turmeric on cancer and inflammation. Almost all chronic diseases are problems with inflammation. Instead of reaching for the painkillers that could blow out your kidneys, when inflammation rears its fire-spitting dragon head, douse it with a turmeric latte. I have used turmeric for joint pain when I first started my diet and lifestyle change, and it worked well. I would steep three tablespoons of dried coriander leaves, a dash of black pepper, and one tablespoon of turmeric powder in a one-litre teapot. I added coconut cream or goat milk and drank it twice daily. I was amazed at the speed of relief I felt on waking.

THE POWER OF CLOVES

A combination of cloves, rosemary and thyme works well for toothaches. I tested the recipe on my son who was a teenager at the time when he had toothaches that kept him awake. He is aware that painkillers are prohibited in our home; so he hid his stash, but when the pain became unbearable, depriving him of sweet sleep, I got to know about the problem. I brought the combination of herbs to a boil, added a pinch of salt to preserve the solution, and gave it to him to drink. According to him, the home remedy worked within an hour. He drank the tea and gargled with it consistently till he had the tooth pulled.

I also recommended that a friend with a toothache daily chew on three pieces of clove for pain relief, she called me back to thank me!

THE POWER OF ONIONS

I used onions to treat a stubborn cough in my granddaughter. I heard Barbara O'Neil, a naturopath discuss home remedies she used on her children when they were growing up. It sounded crazy, but when the time came, I found it very useful and effective (*https://www.youtube.com/watch?v=ptHKWYkaQZE*).

I sliced onions; placed them on her soles, and held them in place with socks throughout the day. Her night coughs subsided and in the morning she awoke cough-free. I am still amazed at the efficacy that something as inconsequential as an onion did the magic where over-the-counter cough syrup had failed us

THE POWER OF VITAMIN E (PALM OIL)

It's been often said that if you want to hide something from a black man hide it in a book. I didn't understand the value of palm oil till I cracked open a book. I used to think that palm oil would cause high cholesterol, and cooked mostly with corn oil. . In 2012, I began feeling tightness on the left side of my chest, between the collar bone and upper part of my breast. Whenever I moved my left arm, a pinching sensation would rip through my chest so I started taking one aspirin daily to ease the discomfort. Whenever I applied pressure to the area, I felt a dull sensation of pain, but was able to manage my symptoms, and kept on with life. In 2016, I bought a book on natural remedies for heart health; not until I read that palm oil is an antioxidant that protects against heart disease was I able to finally knock out the pinching sensation in my chest. I reintroduced palm oil into my diet, following the recommended dosage of two tablespoons daily; to my amazement, my symptoms completely eased to the point that I have forgotten that I ever had such a problem.

THE POWER OF GARLIC

I had problems with my crown after keeping it in for twenty-eight years, and my dentist advised that I had to pull the tooth and replace it with a denture. However, the area of my gum above the affected crown had become infected and needed treating, so the dentist wrote me a five-day antibiotic prescription. My objections fell on deaf ears because my dentist dogmatically believed nothing other than the antibiotic could clear up the infection. I already understood the importance of the microbiome and how a healthy population of bacteria is essential for wellness and decided against wiping out what was left of my friendly gut bacteria against the advice of the expert. I walked past the pharmacy on my way home, the prescription note shoved somewhere in my handbag. Instead, I used a half teaspoon of powdered garlic with lemon juice twice daily for five days. Garlic is a powerful natural antibiotic. At my next appointment, my dentist was pleased with the effectiveness of the antibiotic, not knowing I never took the pills but took control of my health. It's hard arguing with dogma so why bother?

I would prefer you stay proactive rather than reactive. When symptoms occur, it is our body's way of calling our attention to a state of deficiency or toxicity. For instance, nausea, fatigue, feeling light-headed, could be a salt deficiency, but most likely, such symptoms would make some people rush to see their doctor for a prescription. A headache can be relieved by drinking water, or by resting because the symptom could have been precipitated by several factors. Don't be quick to throw a pill at symptoms. Focus on your health goals and act accordingly; when it comes to health care, you have several options.

If you don't mind managing your symptoms, please by all means reach for over-the-counter medication. You also have the option of booking a doctor's appointment, waiting in line, filling a prescription and religiously chugging those pills.

Another option involves you taking your destiny into your hands by doing your research and participating in your treatment to uproot the problem.

The first step to health that won't cost you anything is fasting. When you fast your body goes to work to flush out toxins that allow the healing process to begin. The body is either busy digesting food, or busy detoxifying. It cannot work simultaneously on digesting food and cleaning the house.

Discuss with your doctor to take a nutrition test amongst other recommended tests to verify the status of vitamins, minerals and trace minerals that you could be deficient in. By treating a deficiency, you inadvertently address a toxicity problem; uprooting all diseases.

> *"Don't wait until you're dying to think about living"* Author Unknown

Overhaul Meals and Plan Ahead

It is often said that if you fail to plan, you plan to fail. This saying should not only apply to our finances, but it should also apply to our health. Health is the first line of wealth because, without it, it is impossible to achieve life goals. The first thing to do is prepare your mind to eat an array of colourful fruits and vegetables. Some diets discourage eating fruit, but proponents of whole foods plant-based diets suggest adding fruit to our diet to benefit from inherent antioxidants in the plants. Different colours proffer various health benefits to different organs in our body.

Red fruits and vegetables protect the heart, prevents cancer and urinary tract infections.

White fruits and vegetables help lower cholesterol; detoxify the body and prevent cancer. It also helps to keep blood pressure healthy.

Blue/purple/black fruit and vegetables contain health-promoting phytochemicals that help fight diseases, and also contains anti-ageing properties needed to keep us youthful for as long as possible.

Yellow/orange fruits and vegetables contain high amounts of cancer-fighting antioxidants. Increased levels of antioxidants in the body are closely associated with a lower risk for heart disease.

Green fruits and vegetables provide the body with immune-boosting vitamin C and B-vitamins essential for health. It promotes healthy skin, and helps reduce the risk of age-related blindness; encourages the self-destruction of pre-cancerous cells.

I was excited to discover purple carrots; pleasantly surprised that they tasted just like regular carrots, which means an addition to my food choices. I have also added many more African indigenous grain and seeds to my grocery list while incorporating foreign plants as well. However, I still prepare my meals the African way with palm nut cream, or oil even though some nutrition expert frown on the use of any kind of oil, however despite the misunderstood negative reviews, palm oil remains a powerful source of vitamin E containing tocopherols and tocotrienols. The world is a global village that flings open culinary doors, offering us many choices and allowing us to enjoy foods and plants from different cultures.

Eliminating junk (carbonated drinks, refined vegetable oils, artificial foods and seasonings, processed foods) is another major step here. To get well it is important to eat foods closer to their natural state. Ignorance is not bliss; knowledge is power. When I was diagnosed with high cholesterol, the first thing I did was throw out my palm oil stew only to later read that it had the most potent form of vitamin E on earth! Palm oil is closer to its natural state than the regular vegetable oils donning store shelves.

This diet change could mean cooking your meals, hiring a steward, or ordering a tailored meal from nutrient conscious chefs. Following a meal plan would also prove effective because it tailors your food shopping and meal preparation. It eliminates the stress of deciding on what to eat and eliminates the need to eat junk since you already have a plan. Eating this way can also help you track your nutrient intake, and monitor what foods augur well with you and the foods that you don't enjoy. It can also help you monitor and tally symptoms with foods. Having this information will aid future food choices, and could make the difference between wellness and ill health.

Sample Meal Plan

A sample meal plan would look something like this:

Pre-breakfast about 8 am
Detox juice, such as apple cider vinegar in warm water, lemon in warm water, or bitter herbs.

Breakfast about 10 am
Fruit, nuts, and seeds.

Lunch about 1 pm
Whole grains and vegetables.

Snack
Herbal tea, or vegetable juice, or any fruit in season.

Dinner between 5-6 pm
Salad, soup, or stew.

Food Combination and Cooking Methods

Zeng Jie, a Chinese nutritionist worked till he was 100 years old. According to him, health maintenance is the best doctor. His diet consisted of 10 % animal protein,

20% fat, and 70% carbohydrates. He recommended eating vegetables with all meals and eating little to no dairy. He died at 110 years old. I have since modelled my eating pattern after his recommendations.

What we do with our whole foods makes the difference between absorption and deficiency. We are not what we eat instead we are what we absorb. Absorption is important because it ensures that we get the much-needed nutrients essential to maintaining wellness. Many continue to wash out the nutrients off their leafy greens. Little wonder they doubt the efficacy of leafy greens as a powerhouse of nutrients for the proper functioning of the body. The thinking is: "I have been eating greens all my life and still got sick". You got sick because you only ate fibre without the nutrients. It is best practice to wash leafy green vegetables before cutting.

Also, some people overcook their meats. Frying and grilling meat tends to produce harmful substances that negatively affect our health and keeps us from properly digesting the meat. It is best practice to either boil the meat till tender, or prepare it medium-rare.

It is common practice to combine chockfull animal proteins with starchy staples; however, doing so usually causes our bodies to produce large amounts of insulin to help drive glucose into the cells. Too much insulin could lead to insulin resistance, a precursor to many ailments. If you must add animal protein to a starchy meal it is best to use it as a seasoning in very small amounts.

When we keep our meals simple, do not over-cook and wash away all the nutrients from our leafy greens, we will be better able to access and benefit from the life-giving minerals, vitamins and phytochemicals of the plant. I have heard many nutritionists say that dis-ease is either a problem of toxicity, or a problem of deficiency, and many of us are indeed deficient, if not deficient and toxic! It is good to know that either way, food and herbal teas can help ameliorate and prevent ailments

It is important to note the following:

1. Starches and vegetables take one to two hours to digest, but hunger pangs can be kept at bay with the addition of healthy fats.
2. Vegetables and animal protein take two to three hours to digest. It is best practice to consume vegetables with animal protein because the fat in the meat will enhance the absorption of nutrients in the vegetables.

3. Meat and fish takes three to four hours to digest
4. Shellfish takes four to eight hours to digest
5. Grains and legumes constitute a complete protein, e.g. rice and beans, rice and groundnut, beans and corn.
6. Animal protein and starchy vegetables do not effectively metabolize, it causes insulin to spike excessively and may lead to insulin resistance e.g. yam and meat, rice and meat, wheat products and meat, chicken, or fish.
7. Vegetables go with everything, e.g. fish, chicken, and beef combine well with leafy greens, cabbage, cucumber, carrots, and so on.
8. Fat and starchy vegetable pair well, e.g. yam with groundnut soup, yam with Egusi, cassava and avocado and palm oil.
9. Fruits are better eaten with nuts, kefir, or yoghurt.

Cooking utensils and cooking methods

1. Cooking utensils with fewer toxins are glass, stainless steel and clay pots. Teflon is not recommended.

2. Avoid microwaving food in plastic. It is recommended that we heat food on the stovetop or in the oven to retain nutrients.
3. If you boil vegetables, do not throw out the water because nutrients leech into the cooking water. It can be used as tea or added to a soup as stock.
4. Steaming vegetables preserves the leaching of nutrients.
5. If you need to blanch leafy greens, you should blanch before cutting to preserve nutrients.

Portion Control Guide

Counting calories can be a chore, especially if you are not eating out of a can or a box, besides; calorie counting is not an effective way to manage a good diet. A Yoruba adage says: "The palm of your hands will never deceive you". Here are a few suggestions:

1. The recommended daily intake of animal protein is equal to your palm. If you are eating more than the size of your palm you are ingesting more than your caloric needs.
2. A portion of vegetables is equal to your fistful. Grabbing hold of leafy greens the size of your fist amounts to one serving. It is recommended

that we eat up to five servings of vegetables daily.
3. A portion of carbohydrates is equal to a cupped hand. The serving of starchy vegetables or grains should be no more than what can fit your hand when cupped.
4. A portion of fat is equal to the size of your thumb.

These simple steps above would make a lot of difference concerning your health; would guarantee the elimination of external and internal toxins, while allowing proper metabolizing of foods for adequate absorption of nutrients. Optimal levels of nutrients ensure good health. Even though it is impossible to avoid toxins altogether (our bodies produce toxins as a natural by-product of daily living; our environment is also riddled with toxins), we are not helpless in the face of toxin assaults. Once we give our bodies the right fuel, it goes to work to heal and maintain wellness.

Always remember that your body is self-healing, self-regenerating, and self-restoring. Good health is your natural state.

BE PROACTIVE

"... nutritional excellence is far more powerful than drugs... targeted nutrition has amazing therapeutic potential to revolutionize health care.."

Joel Fuhrman, M.D.

The above information in the preceding chapters skims the surface when it comes to the power of nutrition to reverse diseases, and maintain wellness; nevertheless, it is a good start. Changing your lifestyle and diet can best be achieved by taking baby steps, one at a time.

Once I understood that my physician could not help me, taking control of my health has been the greatest gift that I have given to myself.

Keeping a food diary greatly helped in monitoring my progress; I was able to eliminate foods that disagree with my metabolism, corresponding symptoms with the effectiveness of herbs, spices and foods. Furthermore, I have also been able to identify and add nutrient-dense African foods to my diet. Improving my diet, I have not needed to visit a doctor in five years. Being proactive has afforded me sweet freedom: freedom from sitting around in a doctor's office waiting for a non-existent elixir; freedom from not having to queue at the pharmacy waiting for a prescription, freedom from not having to log around several bottles of pills, but most of all, the freedom to enjoy a healthful life.

I am passionate about the science of nutrition because my food-experiment journey to wellness has conclusively shown me that nutrition packs a powerful punch. I now understand that as Africans, we have what it takes to help the world when it comes to chronic diseases, and maintaining wellness. Not only are our foods nutritious, but we also have many herbs that can daily be added to the diet for robust health.

Diseases common among Africans, such as strokes, high blood pressure, high cholesterol, high blood pressure, glaucoma, itchy skin, eczema, psoriasis, alopecia (hair loss), fatigue, cracked heels, bad breath, body odour, erectile dysfunction, strokes, obesity, to mention a few are all signs of toxicity or/and deficiency and can be reversed by eating a varied nutrient-dense diet.

Preventing disease onset is cheaper and the wisest choice anyone can make. I will briefly discuss preventive measures in regards to diseases common to Africans, such as stroke, erectile dysfunction, and sleep apnea.

Prevention:
1. Maintain healthy blood pressure by exercising regularly.
2. Cut out added sugar, and processed foods. Added sugar acidifies the body and leads to a toxic build-up of metabolic waste.
3. Eat whole intact grains. Whole grains contain fibre, digest slowly and contain resistant starch that will protect against insulin spikes. It is filling and quells hunger pangs
4. Increase intake of vitamin C that is found in leafy greens and fruit. Vitamin C helps reduce blood clumping that leads to blood clots. Pawpaw, guava, and burnt lime fruit are high in vitamin C
5. Eat essential fatty acids found in nuts and seeds, and fatty fish at least thrice weekly. It helps the body absorb fat-soluble vitamins: A, D, E, and K.

6. Magnesium is also important because it helps lower blood pressure and prevents clotting. It also helps to normalize cholesterol levels and improve insulin resistance.
7. Arganine an amino acid found in nuts and seeds, like pistachios and egusi helps control plaque build-up in blood vessels. The downside to eating arginine-rich foods is that it can exacerbate cold sores and arthritis symptoms. This can be remedied by increasing magnesium and vitamin-rich foods. For instance, egusi and leafy greens.
8. Lower stress and sleep well. Stress increases cortisol, which causes inflammation.
9. Intermittent fasting, which gives the body time to rest and focus on repair.

SUGGESTED MEAL PLAN FOR INSULIN RESISTANCE

Insulin resistance is the "accumulation of fat in the muscle and liver that traps glucose in the blood". It is a common, but unrecognised phenomenon amongst Africans; a precursor to many chronic diseases such as diabetes, high blood pressure, obesity, erectile dysfunction, PCOS (polycystic ovarian syndrome) to mention a few. The physical symptoms include, but are not limited to, abdominal fat (pot bellies), skin tags, and painful joints.

Insulin receptors become dysfunctional over time with the overconsumption of animal protein combined with starch and fatty acids, for instance, meat and starchy vegetables, such as rice, cassava, yam; a sedentary lifestyle, and overeating. It can also be triggered by artificial seasonings that greatly spike insulin. For these reasons, it is suggested that insulin resistance can be reversed by eating less animal protein, more fruits, nuts and seeds; leafy greens, intact whole grains, herbs and spices; intermittent fasting, and exercise.

There are many available diets, but to keep things simple, we'll focus on eating a healthy varied diet, and intermittent fasting. The fasting periods will allow the body to rest from producing insulin. Positive signs of insulin sensitivity are lower hunger, lower abdominal fat, increased energy, satiation; improved blood pressure and blood sugar.

Based on personal experience, my knowledge of nutrient-dense African foods, intermittent fasting and exercise, I believe you will attain healthy body weight and reverse insulin resistance. However, remember to throw out the processed foods, carbonated drinks, added sugars, and unhealthy cooking oils.

Nutrient Profile: B-vitamins, vitamins C, A, D, E, and K. Fibre, potassium, chromium, magnesium, and zinc. Please note that the food sources are not exhaustive. I have placed more emphasis on African foods, and if you live in the diaspora, you have access to local and international variety of crops.

Food Sources

Whole Grains: African rice, finger and pearl millet, fonio, sorghum.

Beans and Pulses: Cowpea, kidney beans, black beans, pinto beans, lablab, chickpeas, pigeon peas.

Vegetables: Yams, carrots, cabbage, cassava, plantain, garden eggs, native potatoes, leafy greens, onions, garlic, tomatoes, chillies, beetroot.

Nut and Seeds: Egusi, dika nut, sesame seeds, African walnuts, bitter kola, groundnuts, coconuts, cashews, chestnuts, almonds.

Fruits: Guava, papaya (paw-paw), pineapple, mangoes, watermelon, oranges, banana, jack fruit, soursop, berries, burnt lime fruit, grapefruit, tamarind and avocado.

Teas and Beverages: Lemongrass, cacao, sorghum stalks, chamomile, peppermint, hibiscus flower, bitter melon, mango leaf, soursop.

Herbs and spices: Cloves, thyme, rosemary, parsley, selim seeds, locust beans, turmeric, alligator pepper, cardamom, black pepper, ginger, African nutmeg, cinnamon, mint, Aidan fruit.

Mushrooms: Oyster, chestnut, white button.

Fermented Foods: Sourdough bread, cabbage, sorghum, pearl and finger millet.

Fats: Palm nut cream, coconut oil, butter from grass-fed animals.

24-Hour Fasting Meal Plan

On Waking: Warm water with salt/ lemon/ lime; or apple cider vinegar.

Day 1

Breakfast: Fast day (water, or herbal tea)
Lunch: Fast day (vegetable juice, vegetable broth)
Dinner: Fruit in season (tamarind)
        Stewed beans, corn, and leafy greens
        Herbal tea, or fermented hibiscus tea

Day 2

Breakfast: Fruit in season (Mango)
Finger millet porridge, nut milk, and dates

Lunch: Fruit in season (Berries)
Organ meat suya, cabbage, carrots, lettuce, cucumber, avocado
Peppermint tea

Dinner: Moin-moin (steamed ground beans)/Chakalaka
Sautéed leafy greens, carrots, onions and garlic
Fermented hibiscus tea

Day 3

Breakfast: Fast day (water, or herbal tea)
Lunch: Fast day (vegetable juice, vegetable broth)
Dinner: Fruit in season (Papaya)
Fonio Jollof/foxtail millet, leafy greens, and bell peppers
Herbal tea

Day 4

Breakfast: Fruit in season (Orange)
Pearl millet (nut milk, sesame seeds), dates

Lunch:	Fruit in season (Pineapple) Grilled fish with suya seasoning, leafy green salad Mango leaf tea
Dinner:	Baked native potato, groundnut soup, raw leafy greens Fermented tea, or vegetable juice

Day 5

Breakfast:	Fast day (water, coffee, or herbal tea)
Lunch:	Fast day (vegetable juice, vegetable broth)
Dinner:	Fruit in season (Guava) Stewed cabbage with okra, African rice Fermented hibiscus tea

Day 6

Breakfast:	Fruit (Tamarind) Green smoothie (leafy greens, nut milk, moringa powder, sesame)
Lunch:	Fruit (Papaya) Baked chicken, cucumber-beet salad Peppermint tea
Dinner:	Yam pottage, sautéed kale, onions, and garlic Lemongrass tea

Day 7

Breakfast: Fast day (water, coffee, or herbal tea)
Lunch: Fast day (vegetable juice, or vegetable broth)
Dinner: Mashed boiled yam in tomato sauce
Sautéed kale, mushrooms, onions and garlic
Chamomile tea

Nut Milk Options

1. Toasted egusi and sesame seeds.
2. Blanched groundnuts and sesame seeds.
3. Cashew nuts and sesame seeds.
4. Hemp seeds and sesame seeds.
5. Blanched almond nuts and sesame seeds

SUGGESTED MEAL PLAN FOR AUTO-IMMUNE DISEASES

Autoimmune diseases occur when the immune system attacks healthy cells in the body. Diseases such as multiple sclerosis, arthritis, alopecia; asthma, psoriasis, lupus, eczema, type 1 diabetes, are some common examples. There are no known cures for these disorders, but they are managed with pharmaceutical drugs that can be toxic to the liver over time. These diseases are chronic and become progressively worse if not properly managed. However, there are anecdotal pieces of evidence of people who have reversed their conditions with nutrition.

With auto-immune disorders, the goal is to calm the immune system so that healing can take place; for this to happen certain foods have to be eliminated from the diet. The two major foods to be eliminated are dairy and gluten. "Casein in milk is associated with a prevalence of multiple sclerosis and schizophrenia in twenty-seven countries and twenty-nine populations". While "gluten and casein are associated with early onset of schizophrenia and Parkinson's".

Adding cruciferous and sulphur rich foods to the diet have shown to be effective. Foods such as cabbage, which is a rich source of vitamin k1 helps in myelin production, provides magnesium and carotenoids that help drive calcium into the bones and teeth where they are most needed. Foods such as onions, garlic, and leeks help the body detoxify harmful substances impeding healing. They also help produce glutathione, our body's natural antioxidant; are neuro-protective, and help with endothelial function. Mushrooms are rich in beta-glucan and activate our innate immunity killer cells, while all coloured foods help the body quench the activity of free radicals. Fermented foods are also essential for healing because they help repopulate our microbiome with healthy bacteria that produce short-chain fatty acids.

"Food is so much powerful than supplements"
Terry Wahl, MD

https://www.youtube.com/watch?v=ZVqnjAvl8jY

Nutrient profile: Vitamin C, B12, B1, B6, K2, folate; omega 3 fatty acids, sulphur rich foods.

Food sources

Fruits: Berries, Burnt lime fruit, Lemon, Limes, Pineapples, and Oranges.

Vegetables: Carrots, cabbage, onions, mushrooms, celery, pumpkin leaves, amaranth leaves, rocket, mustard greens, romaine lettuce, red beets, cucumbers, radishes, tomatoes, red bell peppers, yam, cassava, avocado.

Fermented foods: locust beans, African oil bean, melon seeds, nut/seeds yoghurts.

Raw Dairy: Raw goats milk/kefir

Meats: 6-12 ounces of liver, weekly, organ meats (grass-fed only)

Nuts and Seeds: Sesame seeds, black seeds (Nigella Sativa), peanuts, walnuts, Brazil nuts, chia seeds.

Grains: African rice, fermented Sorghum, finger and pearl millet, sourdough bread.

Sweeteners: Raw Honey.

Fats and Oils: Palm oil, coconut oil, extra virgin olive oil.

Herbs and Spices: Sea salt, turmeric, black pepper, ginger, oregano, basil, hibiscus flowers, cloves, calabash nutmeg, selim seeds.

Please try to ensure that all or most of the produce you buy are organic; where you can't buy organic produce, wash vegetables with baking soda and vinegar.

Walk to get fresh air for thirty minutes to one hour before breakfast.

On waking: a glass of water with a pinch of sea salt, or freshly squeezed citrus juice.

16:8-Hour Intermittent Fasting Meal Plan

Day 1

Breakfast: Grapefruit, Finger millet with kefir, nuts of choice.
Chai tea/turmeric latte

Lunch: Pineapple
Leafy green salad, fatty fish sautéed in onions, scallion, and leeks
Hibiscus tea

Dinner: African rice, mushroom pepper sauce with 2 tablespoons palm oil.
Salad (cucumber, carrots, romaine lettuce, and rocket)
Ginger tea

Day 2

Breakfast: Berries, Sorghum porridge, sesame seeds, a handful of nuts
Chocolate-chai beverage

Lunch: 2 Kiwi fruit
Cabbage, Okra-leafy green gumbo, liver
Sorghum stalk-Hibiscus tea

Dinner: Stewed beans with baked plantain

Kale and onion mix
Vegetable juice

Day 3

Breakfast: Grapefruit
Pearl millet porridge, chia seeds, handful nuts
Peppermint tea

Lunch: Paw-paw (Papaya)
Aubergine/yam flour, bean soup, jute leaf, mushrooms
Vegetable juice

Dinner: Salad (lettuce, avocado, carrots, rocket)
Sardines, cashew nut dressing
Lemongrass and ginger tea

Day 4

Breakfast: Mango
Plantain-peanut porridge, chai-spice tea

Lunch: Orange
Leafy green salad (celery, cucumber, spinach, rocket, onions)
Cashew nut dressing
Hibiscus tea

Dinner: Stewed beans and African rice, mushroom stew
Cabbage-carrot-beets slaw
Vegetable juice

Day 5

Breakfast: Green smoothie, kefir, and nuts
Lunch: Pineapple
Organ meats-egusi pepper soup
Lemongrass tea
Dinner: Grilled plantain, stewed beans
Cabbage-carrot mix
Vegetable juice

Day 6

Breakfast: Berry-beet smoothie, nuts and sesame seeds
Chai-turmeric latte beverage
Lunch: Pearl millet flatbread, stewed beans/lentils, organ meats
Kale, mushroom, onion mix
Vegetable juice
Dinner: Orange
Native potatoes, stewed cabbage, leafy greens
Lemongrass tea

Day 7

Breakfast: Tamarind
Sorghum porridge, nut milk, sesame seed

Lunch: Pineapple
African rice and beans, mushroom stew
Sautéed kale, onions, leeks
Sorghum stalk-Hibiscus tea

Dinner: Pearl millet flatbread, stewed beans and cabbage
Spinach, red leaf lettuce
Vegetable juice

SUGGESTED MEAL PLAN FOR CHRONIC KIDNEY DISEASE

The kidneys are vital organs responsible for filtering the blood and removing waste from the body, therefore must especially be cared for. It is important to eliminate from the diet high insulin stimulating foods that acidify the body:

1. All processed foods
2. All artificial sweeteners and seasonings, and processed seasoning in a cube or powdered form.

3. Poultry
4. Meat
5. Bread
6. Sugar
7. Dairy (fresh and canned)
8. Carbonated drinks and beverages

To improve kidney function the following steps are essential:

1. Eat foods that can help restore blood vessels.
2. Eat foods that can help clean out the kidneys.
3. Stay clear of foods that create a lot of metabolic waste, e.g. meat, shellfish, pork.
4. Eat balanced meals low in potassium and phosphorous.
5. Intermittent fasting.
6. Drink plenty of water.
7. Get adequate sunlight
8. Rest, sleep for at least seven hours
9. Exercise.
10. Eat a vegetarian diet with plenty of raw leafy greens and whole grains.

Food sources:

Whole grains: Sorghum, pearl and finger millet, African rice, corn.

Fruit: Lime, lemon, grapefruit, mango, pineapple, dates

Vegetables: Pumpkin leaves, parsley, celery, beetroot, mushrooms, garlic, onions, cabbage, garden eggs, native potatoes

Nut and seeds: Tigernut, dika nut, egusi, groundnuts, sesame seeds

Herbs and spices: Ginger, turmeric, black pepper, cinnamon, guava leaf

Pulses: Beans, lentils

Water

Please note that intermittent fasting requires that meal be consumed within an 8-hour time frame. For instance, breakfast at 10 am, and last meal for the day at 6 pm, or breakfast at noon and last meal at 8 pm, breakfast at 8 am and last meal at 4 pm.

Suggested Meal Plan

Day 1

Breakfast: Grapefruit
Sorghum porridge, Tiger-nut milk, 2 dates, a handful of groundnuts
Ginger and lime

Lunch:	Pineapple chunks Mushroom stew, African rice and beans, raw leafy greens Ginger and lime tea
Dinner:	Beans and corn, leafy greens (pumpkin leaves) water and lime

Day 2

Breakfast:	Mango Sorghum porridge, cinnamon, nuts, 2 dates, tiger-nut milk. Ginger and lime tea
Lunch:	grapefruit Sweet potato, leafy green vegetable sauce, garden eggs (raw) Lemonade
Dinner:	Stewed cabbage, mushroom and vegetable soup Ginger tea

Day 3

Breakfast: Smoothie (Tiger-nut milk, leafy greens, nuts, ginger, cinnamon)

Lunch:	Grapefruit Native potato and beans, leafy greens

	Water
Dinner:	Paw-paw (Papaya)
	African rice, raw leafy greens, garden eggs (raw)
	Stewed mushrooms
	Ginger- guava tea.

A Korean naturopath put a patient on this diet of whole grains and leafy greens and significantly reversed the patient's disease. Creatine levels dropped from 4.2-1.7, and renal function rose from 14%-70% within three months of following the diet. He discourages consuming animal protein, stressing that kidney stones can develop when it is combined with folate. For more information, he can be reached at kiim36@naver.com

Since Kidney disease is progressively regressive, it is important to work with a professional health care provider.

IMMUNE BOOSTING DIET

The immune system is a complex subject that even 'experts' are still grappling with, therefore to keep the body optimally functioning it is best to eat a varied diet, fast intermittently, and exercise. Below are some key nutrients essential for optimal functioning:

Vitamin D is a hormone derived mainly through our skin's exposure to the sun; otherwise, it can be derived through supplementation. It is responsible for modulating our immune system, protects us from over 40 different diseases.

Zinc is essential for the proper functioning of the immune system and helps skin structure.

Vitamin A is essential for healthy skin and eyesight.

Vitamin C is needed for healthy skin development, and is also essential for the immune system and helps the body absorb iron.

Magnesium is essential in helping the body in absorbing and breaking down other minerals and vitamins. With low levels of magnesium, nothing else works.

Food sources for Zinc: Egusi seeds, tiger nuts, dark chocolate, garlic, sorghum, sesame seeds, watermelon, chickpeas, coconut water, guava, mushrooms, leafy greens, pomegranates, kiwi, nuts, avocado.

Meat, fish, lamb; organic chicken.

Food sources for Vitamin A: Sweet potatoes, Carrots, Kale, Papaya, Green peas, Mangoes, Red bell peppers, Tomatoes. Liver, Egg yolks, Fatty fish, Organic butter, Cod liver oil, Cheese.

Food sources of Vitamin C: Guava, burnt lime fruit, lemons, broccoli, Brussel sprouts, beef brain, liver, goat milk, cauliflower, hibiscus flowers, bell peppers.

"Put the focus on food quality and healthy lifestyle practices to attain a healthy weight" (Harvard Women's Health. October 2020)

Food Combination Samples:

Starchy Vegetables and Leafy Greens

Yam Po-po
Ingredients: puna yam, tomatoes, red bell pepper, mushrooms, onions, oregano, palm oil, salt and chillies.

Spicy Coconut Mogo
Ingredients: cassava, coconut milk, tomatoes, onions, birds eye chillies, shredded carrots, African oil bean, kale, and oyster mushrooms

Potato Casserole

Ingredients: potatoes, chickpeas, tomatoes, red bell peppers, onions, coriander

Egusi Stew with Chia-infused Garri

Ingredients: Stew: egusi, birds eye chillies, palm oil, locust beans, oyster mushrooms, palm oil, smoked herring.

Garri: roasted cassava flakes, chia seeds.

Egusi-Peanut Soup with Sourdough Bread

Ingredients: egusi, peanuts, garden eggs, palm oil, African birds eye chillies, coriander.

Animal Protein and Vegetables

Sunny Side Eggs and Vegetables

Ingredients: sunny side eggs, red bell peppers, onions, mushrooms, spinach, sauteed in palm oil.

Dika Nut Soup with Cabbage Dough

Ingredients: dika nut, palm oil, cauliflower, mushrooms, liver, cabbage bound with psyllium husk (cabbage dough). Seasoned with locust bean, salt and pepper

Grilled Chicken and Cabbage

Ingredients: oven grilled chicken and mushrooms, cabbage, carrots, onions, scotch bonnet peppers, turmeric and black pepper sautéed in palm oil.

Snails

Fish

Legumes and Grains

African Rice with Bambara Nut, Salad bowl, Avocado

Ingredients: Rice dish (African rice, bambara nut, palm oil, onions, tomatoes, red bell peppers. Salad (red onions, cucumber, red bell peppers, tomatoes, lemon juice)

Millet and Beans with Salad

Ingredients: foxtail millet, chickpeas, palm oil stew.

Stewed Beans and Corn

Ingredients: pinto beans, sweet corn, tomatoes, onions, red bell peppers, palm oil.

Ethiopian Barley and Pearl Millet Porridge with Berries

Ingredients: pearl millet, peanut milk, dates, cinnamon, cherries, black berries,

Vegetables and Legumes

Harira Soup

Ingredients: red split lentils, chickpeas, onions, tomatoes, parsley, oregano, salt and black pepper

Steamed Beans (Olele), Salad, and Porridge

Olele (Moin-moin), salad, and porridge.

Ingredients: Salad (shredded cabbage, beetroot, purple carrot, orange carrot)

Olele (cowpea beans, kale, green chillies, green sweet peppers, peanut oil, salt and pepper)

Porridge (Finger millet, cooked with sorghum stalks and dates, topped with peanut milk)

Plantain and Sukuma Wiki

Ingredients: Sukuma wiki (kale, onion, sautéed in peanut oil.)

Plantain fried in palm oil, Mushrooms in tomato sauce

EAT TO HEALTH AND WELLNESS ON AN AFRICAN DIET

Steamed Lentils

Ingredients: red split lentils, onions, red bell pepper, raw peanuts, sesame seeds. Seasoned with salt and white pepper.

Salad (cucumber, rocket/arugula

Beans and Plantain (Chakalaka)

Ingredients: cabbage, carrots, onion. Stewed beans and corn, plantain

Vegetables and Grains

African rice, Stewed Mushrooms, and Kale

Ingredients: African rice, tomatoes, onions, red bell pepper, red chillies, mushrooms, kale.

Raw African Rice

Sautéed Okra with Rice and Chickpeas

Ingredients: Okra, onions, red bell peppers, scotch bonnet.

Basmati rice, brown chickpeas cooked in Ethiopian doro wot.

Ezekiel Bun Burger

Ingredients: Ezekiel bun, mushrooms and onions sautéed in palm oil, spinach and avocado, seasoned with salt and black pepper.

Vegetables

Green Monster

Ingredients: parsley, celery, green peppers, spinach, nut milk.

Onions and Spinach

Ingredients: butter, onions, spinach and scotch bonnet peppers.

Purple Carrots

Ingredients: carrots

Simple Salad

Ingredients: cucumber and spinach

Kachumbari

Ingredients: tomatoes, red onions, cucumber, red bell peppers, lemon juice

Mushroom Vegetable Mix

Ingredients: Mushrooms, onions, kale, tomatoes, scotch bonnet, palm oil seasoned with Suya spice.

Tomatoes

Beverages

Hibiscus Flower and Sorghum Hot Tea

Ingredients: hibiscus flowers, sorghum stalks, pineapple, cloves, ginger

Cold Zobo

Ingredients: hibiscus flowers, cloves, pineapple

Herbal Tea

Ingredients: Lemon grass, oregano, thyme, and bay leaf

Turmeric Beverage

Ingredients: coconut milk, turmeric, black pepper, dates, nutmeg.

Ginger and Lime Smoothie

Ingredients: ginger, lime, spinach, coconut water

Fruits, Nuts and Seeds

Nut Bar
Ingredients: walnuts, pecans, cashews, raw cacao, sesame seeds, dates, cinnamon, dried mango.

Nut Milk
Ingredients: almonds, peanuts, sesame seeds, and dates

Peanut-Sesame Yogurt with Fruit

Ingredients: peanuts, sesame seeds, cinnamon.

Kunun Tsamiya

Ingredients: tamarind, pearl millet, dates

Sorghum Porridge with Chia Seeds and Nut Yogurt

Ingredients: fermented sorghum, chia seeds, dates, peanut yogurt

Sugar Cane Juice

Ingredients: sugar cane

Avocado Smoothie

Ingredients: avocado, spinach, ginger, peanut yogurt, dates and water

CONCLUSION

I share the hope and aspirations of many chiropractors, homoeopaths, and naturopaths I dream that someday in the nearest future doctors will treat chronic ailments with nutrition instead of throwing pills at them. I have tried to compress a nine-year journey into a few chapters to help those who are tired of daily chugging a handful of pills with little hope in sight. Even though diet and lifestyle change is hard, once you realize that food is your best medicine, you will be motivated to make the switch to save your life. I was inspired to share my experiences with you because of the health progress I have made, and because of inspiring stories I have read and heard throughout the years. I hope that this book will do you a lot of good, and subsequently help you attain health and wellness so that you won't need a physician.

I am aware that within the African culture adding meat to every meal and eating meat as a snack is a usual practice, which might make the switch to a predominantly plant-based diet difficult.

One useful tip is to predetermine the days to add animal protein to meals. For instance, I tend to eat animal protein in small amounts on Mondays, Wednesdays, and Fridays. If there is a family gathering, I might eat some animal protein on Saturdays, or Sundays. I also try to ensure that I combine my animal protein with a mix of cabbage, mushrooms, and leafy greens.

Mushrooms and eggplants are great substitutes for meat. Some Africans in the diaspora substitute cauliflower or organic tofu for meat in their stews and have said they didn't miss the meat! A tribe in the South-West of Nigeria substitute green hibiscus flowers for meat in their Egusi soup.

Another difficulty to contend with whenever we make a diet change is cravings. Cravings could be an indication that the body is missing something, or it could simply be due to the force of habit. According to Eric Berg, cravings differ and point to different deficiencies. In his view, a meat craving could be a bile deficiency, so starting the day with bitter herbs like dandelion root tea, apple cider vinegar, or garlic might help the body better digest and absorb fat-soluble vitamins-
https://www.youtube.com/watch?v=n4Ld_fI7-SU

Also regularly adding nuts and seeds to your diet will help with satiety, which would invariably reduce cravings. Adding more legumes to your diet, prepared in different ways, will provide your body with fibre to keep you full.

Our bodies are designed in such a way that we're either digesting food or repairing cells, so it is advisable to eat only when hungry and refrain from snacking. Eating a full meal to satiety will surely help with cravings.

I hope you are motivated to take the steps necessary to see desired changes that will lead you into health and wellness.

Always remember that health is your natural state, and without health, there is no freedom.

Olayinka Flo Falana
2021

REFERENCES

1. Paavo Airola, PhD. 'How To Get Well'. Dr. Airola's Handbook of Natural Healing.
2. Dr. Jason Fung, 'The Cancer Code'. A revolutionary understanding of a medical mystery.
3. Russ Brandon, '25 Superfoods That Naturally Lower High Blood Pressure'
4. Joseph Moss, 'Blood Pressure, How to Lower it Fast'
5. Agora Health, '259 All-Natural Secrets To Disease-Proof Your Heart, Unclog Your Arteries And Keep Your Ticker Ticking Stronger Than Someone Half Your Age'
6. Joel Fuhrman, M.D. 'The End of Diabetes'. The Eat To Live Plan To Prevent and Reverse Diabetes
7. Dr. William Li, 'Eat To Beat Disease'. The body's five defence systems and the foods that could save your life.

8. Joel Fuhrman, M.D. 'Fast Food Genocide' How Processed Food is killing Us and What We Can Do About It.

9. Rose Michaels, 'Spice Mixes', Your Complete Seasoning Cookbook

10. Eric Berg, D.C. Youtube,

11. John Bergman, D.C. Youtube

12. Terry Wahls, M.D. Youtube

13. National Research Council, 2008. Lost Crops of Africa. Volume III: Fruits, Washington, D.C: The National Academic Press

14. National Research Council, 2008. Lost Crops of Africa. Volume I: Grains, Washington, D.C: The National Academic Press

15. National Research Council, 2008. Lost Crops of Africa. Volume II: Vegetables, Washington

16. https://www.youtube.com/watch?v=a6fOvTujkEA

17. https://www.youtube.com/watch?v=DgJH50ifMxs

18. https://www.youtube.com/watch?v=regx1R1yz0A

Printed in Great Britain
by Amazon